At a Breezy Time of Day

Other Books of Interest from St. Augustine's Press

James V. Schall, *The Sum Total of Human Happiness*

James V. Schall, *The Regensburg Lecture*

James V. Schall, *The Modern Age*

James V. Schall, *The Classical Moment:*
Selected Essays on Knowledge and Its Pleasures

James V. Schall, *The Praise of 'Sons of Bitches':*
On the Worship of God by Fallen Men

James V. Schall, *Docilitas:*
On Teaching and Being Taught

James V. Schall, *On the Principles of Taxing Beer:*
And Other Brief Philosophical Essays

James V. Schall, *Remembering Belloc*

Marc D. Guerra (editor), *Jerusalem, Athens, & Rome:*
Essays in Honor of James V. Schall

Marc D. Guerra, *Liberating Logos:*
Pope Benedict XVI's September Speeches

Robert Royal (editor), *The Catholic Thing:*
Five Years of a Singular Website

Joseph Pearce (editor), *Beauteous Truth:*
Faith, Reason, Literature and Culture

Peter Kreeft, *Summa Philosophica*

Peter Kreeft, *The Sea Within*

Josef Pieper, *What Does "Academic" Mean?:*
Two Essays on the Chances of the University Today

Josef Pieper, *Enthusiasm and Divine Madness*

Josef Pieper, *Don't Worry about Socrates*

Roger Scruton, *The Politics of Culture and Other Essays*

Roger Scruton, *An Intelligent Person's Guide to Modern Culture*

Barry Cooper, *Consciousness and Politics*

At a Breezy Time of Day

Selected Schall Interviews on Just about Everything

James V. Schall

ST. AUGUSTINE'S PRESS

South Bend, Indiana

Manufactured in the United States of America.

1 2 3 4 5 6   25 24 23 22 21 20 19

Library of Congress Cataloging in Publication Data
Names: Schall, James V., interviewer.
Title: At a breezy time of day : selected Schall interviews on just about everything / James V. Schall.
Description: 1st [edition].
South Bend, Indiana : St. Augustines Press,
Inc., 2016.
Includes index.
Identifiers: LCCN 2016033730
ISBN 9781587310829 (hardcover : alk. paper)
Subjects: LCSH: Theology.
Catholic Church--Doctrines.
Schall, James
V.--Interviews.
Classification: LCC BX1751.3 .S265 2016
DDC 230/.2--dc23 LC record available at https://lccn.loc.gov/2016033730

∞ The paper used in this publication meets the minimum requirements of the American National Standard for Information Sciences - Permanence of Paper for Printed Materials, ANSI Z39.48-1984.

St. Augustine's Press
www.staugustine.net

"When they heard the sound of the Lord God moving about in the garden *in the breezy time of the day*, the man and his wife hid themselves from the Lord God among the trees of the garden. The Lord then called to the man and asked him, 'Where are you?' He answered, 'I heard you were in the garden, but I was afraid, because I was naked, so I hid myself.' Then He asked, 'Who told you that you were naked? You have eaten then from the tree, of which I had forbidden you to eat!"

—From the World's First Recorded Interview, Genesis, 1, 3:8–11.

ACKNOWLEDGEMENTS

The author wishes to thank the editors of the following sources for permission to reprint interviews that previously had appeared in their publications and blogs:

Chapter 1, the Harvard *Ichthus*; Chapter 2, *Telos* Magazine; Chapter 3, *National Review*; Chapter 4, *Inside Catholic*; Chapter 5, Acton Institute; Chapter 6, *Gilbert Magazine*; Chapter 7, *America Magazine*; Chapter 8, *Ignatius Insight*; Chapter 9, Knoxville *Journal-Express*; Chapter 10, The Georgetown *Hoya*; Chapter 11, *Dominicana*; Chapter 12, *National Catholic Register*; Chapter 13, Zenit; Chapter 14, Belmont Abbey College *Crossroads*; Chapter 15, *The Dartmouth College Apologia*; Chapter 16, *Il Foglio*, Rome; and Chapter 17, *Crux*.

TABLE OF CONTENTS

Introduction   "By the Thinking Part of My Readers"   1
Chapter 1   Interview with Jordan Teti in the Harvard *Ichthus*   5
Chapter 2   Interview with Maxwell Woods in *Telos*   22
Chapter 3   Interview with Kathryn Lopez in
             National Review On-line   25
Chapter 4   Interview with Robert Reilly in
             Inside Catholic On-line   36
Chapter 5   Interview with Acton Institute   52
Chapter 6   Interview with Sean Daily at *Gilbert Magazine*   59
Chapter 7   Interview with Sean Salai
             in *America Magazine* On-Line   66
Chapter 8   Interview with Carl Olson at *Ignatius Insight* on-line   73
Chapter 9   Interview with Perry Bell
             in the Knoxville, Iowa, *Journal-Express*   88
Chapter 10   Interview with Danny Funt
              in *The Hoya*, Georgetown University   93
Chapter 11   Interview with Ignatius Smith
              in *Dominicana* On-line   100
Chapter 12   Interview with Sofia Mason
              in *National Catholic Register*   110
Chapter 13   Interview with Annamarie Adkins in Zenit   113
Chapter 14   Interview with Edward Jones
              in *Crossroads*, Belmont Abbey College   117
Chapter 15   Interview with Christopher Hauser
              in the *Dartmouth College Apologia*   130
Chapter 16   Interview with Matteo Matzuzzi
              in *Il Foglio* On-line   137
Chapter 17   Interview with Interview with Kathryn Lopez
              in *Crux* On-line   142
Conclusion   "The Nearest Notion of Paradise"   153

Introduction

"BY THE THINKING PART OF MY READERS"

"In my *interview* with Dr. Johnson this evening, I (Boswell) was quite easy, quite as his companion; upon which I find in my Journal the following reflection: 'So ready is my mind to suggest matter for dissatisfaction, that I felt a sort of regret that I was so easy. I missed that awful reverence with which I used to contemplate Mr. Samuel Johnson, in the complex magnitude of his literary, moral, and religious character. I have a wonderful superstitious love of *mystery*; when, perhaps, the truth is, that it is owing to the cloudy darkness of my own mind. I should be glad that I am more advanced in my progress of being, so that I view Dr. Johnson with a steadier and clearer eye. My dissatisfaction tonight was foolish. Would it not be foolish to regret that we shall have less mystery in a future state? That we now 'see in a glass darkly,' but we shall then 'see face-to-face!' This reflection, which I thus freely communicate, will be valued *by the thinking part of my readers*, who may themselves have experienced a similar state of mind."
—*Boswell's Life of Johnson*, March 20, 1778, II, 172.

Whether the "interview," like the essay or novel, is a distinct form of literature can be debated. Certainly, the interview format has many good things about it. The interviewer can bring up questions about issues that might not otherwise occur to an author, or issues he did not talk about but should have. The interview format is more open and, in many cases, more revealing. Like Pope Francis' famous interviews, we can be left wondering just what was meant by what was said or not explained. But for the most part, the interview is a welcome form of communication. Interviews usually arise from outside the intentions of the one interviewed. From some newspaper, journal, or on-line site, some interrogator will take the initiative to propose an interview on some specific or general topic. The interviewer assumes that the person with whom he chooses to talk has something to say that is worth recording.

Published interviews usually need some editing. They leave out the grunts and the "ehs," or at least most of them. Sometimes they are worth leaving in. The interview allows a more relaxed, if not a more colloquial, way of speaking, a way that is sometimes more telling and more exact as to what the speaker meant or was understood to be saying. It is "fair game" to inquire of a speaker, professor, politician, or witness just what he intended by something he wrote or commented on. The interview is not exactly like "thinking out loud." but it does bring to the fore what someone might think that would otherwise not be known. We are often not at our clearest when we think that we are most lucid. It is always helpful when someone asks us, "Just what did you mean by this or that statement of yours?"

This book's title, *At a Breezy Time of Day*, comes from what I call "the first recorded interview." It is a playful theme about a pleasant time of day. The Lord goes looking for Adam and Eve. Adam is obviously keeping out of the way. His divine interlocutor wonders, "Why are you hiding?" Notice it is the questions that constitute the "drama" of this famous interview. In a logic that the reader is already suspicious about, the Lord wants to know who told Adam that he was "naked"? Obviously, no one told him. He figured it out himself.

Adam's lack of "costume" was no different before he violated the rule than after. The awareness of his unclad condition in the breezy afternoon was caused by his own choice and its subsequent consequences. The "first" interview did not have the purpose of informing either Adam himself or the Lord that the man had violated the commandment. The inquiry was to inform the man, and those of us who read about him, that the Lord knew the situation. So, pun not necessarily not intended, interviews can, as in the case of Adam, be pretty "revealing" about the human condition. If nothing else, this insight alone would justify their worth.

No doubt, none of the seventeen interviews that follow in these pages has quite the same dramatic setting as "the first recorded interview" on that "breezy" afternoon in the Garden. But the word "breezy" can perhaps indicate both something of the lightsomeness of an interview and something of the fact that such a spirit can touch more serious depths that reach to the heart of things, to things of first importance.

As I suggested in the book's sub-title, the interview can bring up a discussion or reflection on "just about everything." The only reason that anything is left out is probably because no one ever asked a pertinent question in an interview. But not every thought of ours is worth publishing. Still, in an interview one is expected to respond even if he does not know too much about a topic. Nothing is wrong with saying "I don't know" when he doesn't. But opinions are often more revealing than truths. It is not wrong to express them most of the time.

The occasions for the interviews that compose this book vary widely. They are interviews that took place more or less during the recent decade or so. By their topics and the persons to whom they refer, they will reveal their context. We cannot really talk of important things unless we talk of everyday things at the same time. I have not given each interview a separate title. They are identified by their source. I have, however, introduced each interview with a short passage from the interview to follow to give some sense or flavor of what is being discussed.

Someone from out of nowhere will call or send a message that requests an interview. If it sounds like a good topic, one can accept and arrange for a time and place. None of the interviews in this collection was in person. They were the results of exchanges between myself and the one requesting the interview. They were published in journal or on-line form. But collectively, though there will be similarities of themes, they cover many topics of general and specific interest about writing, philosophy, education, politics, theology, individuals, situations, one's life, and general human nature. They need not be read all at once, though it is not a sin to do so. They are probably best read one at a time.

In the beginning of this Introduction, I cited a rather long "interview" of James Boswell concerning his relation to Dr. Samuel Johnson, the great eighteenth-century lexicographer, philosopher, essayist, and sage. In its own way, it is a remarkable passage worth considerable reflection. Boswell has now known Johnson for many years. He has become familiar with his ways and habit of mind. He no longer has the same "awe" of the man that he did in his earlier years. But this is not what bothers Boswell. He is aware of the charm of "mystery," of what we do not know but search for. In referring to St. Paul's famous statement that we will see the Lord "face-to-face," Boswell worries that so seeing will mean that the mystery will disappear.

He wonders whether the "thinking part of his readers" may not be vexed by the same concerns.

So Boswell addresses the "thinking part of mankind" to see if they have similar concerns. Hopefully, these interviews are directed to the same audience. Boswell's concern about there being nothing left to know is a kind of vanity, to be sure. In its logic, it implies that man is a god who is capable of understanding everything so that no mystery remains. Aquinas had already addressed this very issue. The mystery of human intelligence is not that we know nothing, but that of the highest things, we know more of what they are not than of what they are. And yet with Aristotle, we strive to know the little of the divine things that we can know.

From the interview on a breezy afternoon in the Garden, we learn that things happen that ought not to happen on such pleasant days. We also realize that when terrible things happen, of which we are ourselves too often the causes, it is not the end. Things were to come about because of the man's deed that he could not have anticipated. His deed will even come to be called a *felix culpa*, a happy fault. The purpose of an interview is, at bottom, to set things straight, to see where things might fit together and where they do not, why they do not. These interviews usually, as I say, have a lightsome spirit. Good things can also happen on breezy afternoons in our gardens. I hope that at least some of these more worthy things are also touched on in these various interviews.

Chapter 1

"Our existence comes to us not by chance or by necessity, but as a gift and as a project."

Interview by Jordan Teti (JT) with James V. Schall, S.J. (JVS) for *The Harvard Ichthus.**

Question #1: (JT) Did you know there were Christian students at Harvard College? or that they had a journal?

Answer #1: (JVS) On the first query, I strongly suspected so, on the second, negative. I am pleased to know of both. Indeed, by the logic of the question, I am delighted to know "non-Christian" students are found at Harvard! Part of being a Christian has to do with "going forth" and having something important to say to all nations. Being Christian assumes that we do not have to be obnoxious to do the latter, though there are martyrs, including contemporary ones, that tell us it is often a dangerous project. Indeed, the creation of an atmosphere, of institutions and opportunities, for everyone to speak to everyone about fundamental things in relative peace has been the great project of John Paul II and carried on by Benedict XVI, themselves two of the most intellectually stimulating figures in contemporary public life. A most disturbing aspect of the mystery of evil concerns this question: "Why is this effort to speak of the highest things to one another so difficult?"

I have only been on the Harvard campus once, but I do recall the passage in Solzhenitsyn's famous 1978 Commencement Address there during which he cited the college motto—*Veritas*. When I was on the campus, I remember standing before a Gate with the *Veritas* symbol, presumably the

---

* Published in *The Harvard Ichthus: A Student Journal of Christian Thought at Harvard College*, 2 (Spring, 2006).

1875 Gate. I have long been moved by the words about that motto that Solzhenitsyn addressed on that rainy day to Harvard graduates: "Many of you have already found out and others will find out in the course of their lives," the great Russian novelist told them, "that truth eludes us if we do not concentrate with total attention on its pursuit." Such are solemn, moving words that anyone with half a heart would be honored to have addressed to himself, to his college. Conversely, one would hate to have as the epitaph on his tombstone: "Here Lies John Smith, '04: *Truth Eluded Him.*"

The first words in Aquinas's *Summa Contra Gentiles* are "*Veritatem meditabitur guttur meum …*," which words, "My mouth (literally, 'wind-pipe') shall meditate on truth," are taken from Proverbs 8:7. Aquinas observes in the first question of this *Summa*, that "the ultimate end of the universe must be the good of intellect." He adds, "This good is truth." So I do hope students at Harvard College, Christian or otherwise, when they pass through this *Veritas* Gate, do not fail to ponder how this word, *Veritas*, takes them back to the core of their being, indeed to the origins of the universe itself.

Harvard College, from 1636, is the oldest college in this country. Georgetown, from 1789, is the oldest Catholic college. Its roots go back to the founding of the Colony of Maryland in 1634 when English Jesuits first came to this country.

As an aside, I might add here that in front of the lovely Gothic Healy Building on the Georgetown campus is located a statue of a seated John Carroll, of the founding Maryland Carroll family; his brother and cousin signed the Declaration and the Constitution. John Carroll was at the time a "suppressed Jesuit," the Order having been disbanded by the papacy from 1773–1815. Carroll was the first Bishop of Baltimore and the founder of Georgetown.

The statue is said to have been conceived and erected in imitation of the statue of John Harvard on the Harvard campus. In examining the two statues, the sharp eye will notice that the space immediately under Harvard's chair is empty, whereas that under John Carroll is obviously filled in and bronzed over. The reason for this filling-in, according to legend, is that, over the years, the comparatively more undisciplined Georgetown students were recurrently wont to place a chamber pot under the sedentary prelate. The Jesuits of an earlier age had to use a certain craftiness to foil further undergraduate blasphemy! I do not know whether earlier Harvard officials may have had the same problem or whether they solved it by more drastic measures. No doubt modern students find chamber pots more difficult to come by or, perhaps, see such bold use to be less witty.

We have an Argentine Jesuit with us in our community this semester who was until recently the president of the University of Cordoba there. This latter school dates back to 1621 and thus is older than Harvard. Moreover, the Argentine Jesuit, as had his father and grandfather, went to college at the famous Jesuit school at Stoneyhurst in England. Stoneyhurst was originally founded in 1593 at St. Omer's in France during forced exiles of Catholics during the English Reformation. The school only made it to England after the French Revolution in 1794. I understand it is a beautiful place.

I taught for twelve years in the Gregorian University in Rome, the founding of which goes back to 1551. In all of these places, I suspect, students, in one form or another, once attentively reflected on the things found in Plato, Aristotle, Sophocles, Cicero, Seneca, along with the Hebrew Bible and the Christian writers. They knew about Augustine in Carthage, Cyril in Alexandria, Bede in Iona, Aquinas in Paris, and Dante in Florence. I hope university students still reflect on these things even if they are not encouraged to do so. We cannot much know what we are unless we know what we have been. Indeed, on the Harvard *Veritas* Gate are also found the words of Isaiah, 25:2: "Open ye gates that the righteous nation which keepeth the truth may enter in ...."

And, on this topic, thanks for your later e-mail information that the inscription on the 1881 Gate is St. John's famous, "Ye shall know the truth and the truth shall make ye free." You tell me that the original motto of Harvard was *Veritas Christo et Ecclesiae,* something that wisely appears untranslated in the identification box of your student journal, "Truth for Christ and the Church."

Such original things should be kept in stone to be remembered, even when one's university drops part of its motto. At first it looked to me like the case endings in that Latin phrase are wrong. I thought it should have read, *Veritas Christi et Ecclesiae*, the truth of Christ and of the Church, both genitives. Then, on looking it up, one source said that the original motto was: *Veritas pro Christo et Ecclesia,* the study of truth "in behalf of" or "for the good of" or "through the inspiration of" Christ and the Church.

By way of further introduction, I cite these sundry local signs of what we are about, hopefully wherever we are—to meditate on truth, to keepeth it through all the turmoil of the nations that such schools have seen, to know how the end of the universe is intellect and its good is the truth itself, that it is truth which makes us free, that this truth is, finally, the Word, Person. *Veritas Christi et Ecclesiae, Veritas pro Christo et Ecclesia, Veritas Christo et Ecclesiae.*

Q. #2): (JT) Many people, whether religious or not, have a hard time seeing how reason could have anything to do with faith, or a belief in the "incredible." Some scholars today (in the sciences, for example) talk about how important verification is in order for us to ground convictions. But what are the essential ways in which faith *can* intersect with reason?

A. #2): (JVS) First of all, this is a recurrent question that appears in every generation and in most cultures. I have dealt with it, in one way or another, as their titles indicate, in all my political philosophy books—*The Politics of Heaven & Hell; Reason, Revelation, and the Foundations of Political Philosophy; At the Limits of Political Philosophy; Roman Catholic Political Philosophy;* and *Jacques Maritain, The Philosopher in Society.* Its terms have to be understood.

Neither the word "faith" nor "reason" is totally unambiguous in actual usage. The first task of intellect is to clarify what exactly we are talking about when we use such terms. We need to state what a thing is and affirm or deny that it is. If you call a potato a banana and I call a banana a potato, until we decide what is what, we will have considerable difficulty in determining over what to pour the gravy. This pouring, to be sure, assumes in our culture that we both call gravy "gravy," so that we do not subsequently pour gravy over bananas.

Men have thought about this issue of faith and reason almost since the beginning so that we ought not to presume to talk about it as if we were the first people who ever broached the topic. But it is still ours to reflect on even if Aristotle explained it all, and he in fact explained an astonishing amount. Some things we need to think about ourselves even if nobody or everybody else also thinks about them. The perfection of intellect is also our perfection, no one else's. And this perfection is, finally, to know the truth of *what is.* The great Socratic enterprise of knowing ourselves begins with the knowing of what is not ourselves and, I suppose, with the being grateful that there is not only ourselves to know.

Take the word "incredible." Strictly speaking if faith itself is incredible, it means that under no circumstances can it be believed, let alone understood. Christian faith does not understand "incredible" in this sense. The two most famous statements on the topic—*fides quaerens intellectum* and *credo ut intelligam*—are designed precisely to affirm that there is something intelligible about faith and something in revelation that is also aimed at intellect.

Faith and reason are not opposed as what is intelligible to what is in no way intelligible. Faith and reason are intended to go together as two ways to know the same ultimate truths about the same common cosmos. We do not have two "worlds," one of faith and one of reason, neither of which is related to the other. Rather we have one world, knowable, according to the nature of each way of knowing, both by faith and by reason. We need to add that, according to the Christian faith, the world itself need not exist. It does not explain its own existence, but it does indicate that it does need explaining. God would be God even if the world did not exist. This implies, ultimately, that we are not solely products of cosmic or chaotic necessity but of a divine freedom and joy.

The problem with faith, if there is one, is not that it is irrational or unbelievable, but that our intellects, though truly intellects, are not the highest forms of intellect in the universe. For something to be "beyond" the power of my intellect does not mean that it is therefore unreasonable or unintelligible as such. It only means that Schall's intellect is not powerful enough to see the scope of things in which the matter at issue becomes clear. Otherwise, if Schall insists that everything must be known first and foremost by Schall's intellect, it follows logically that Schall is putting in a divine claim for his own mind. One ought, presumably, to be reasonably skeptical about such a claim. Aquinas noted this distinction when he said that some things are knowable in themselves, others are known first to us. From the latter we proceed to the former.

Q. #3): (JT) Are faith and reason the same as reason and revelation?

A. #3): (JVS) Such questions, I think, are better posed in terms of reason and revelation, rather than faith and reason. Faith or trust means the acceptance of something as true on the authority of another. Most of the things we do or make or know in everyday life, in fact, we know by authority, that is, by the testimony or guidance of someone who knows. Ultimately, no such thing exists as faith that is simply in yet another act of faith, *ad infinitum*. All faith, by its own logic, finally depends on the testimony of someone who sees the truth or the fact at issue. The problem of faith is rather, "Is this witness credible?" That is, is he telling me what he knows? Every revealed doctrine that is to be accepted by faith is rooted in someone who, on feasible grounds, sees its truth and testifies to it.

Basically, revelation is directed to reason. Aquinas, knowing the essential outlines of the content of revelation (one does not have to be a believer to know what this content is, anyone can read the *General Catechism*), proceeds to ask, "Is this revelation 'necessary'?" (I-II, 91, 4). The word "necessary" here means rather "persuasive." Aquinas does not think, nor does any sound Christian, that one can argue directly from reason to the truths of revelation. If he could perform this intellectual feat of seeing the divine truths with the human mind, he would already be God and would not have to worry his head about it.

The question is rather this: Certain things are found in revelation—basically, that there is an inner-Trinitarian life within the Godhead and that one of the Persons of this Trinity became Man, at a given time and place. Are there any issues within reason that might indicate that this revealed understanding of reality might best correspond with issues that the human mind by itself did not figure out, but still wondered about?

What is characteristic particularly of Catholicism is a concern for philosophy as itself necessary to understand properly the meaning of revelation. Leo Strauss mentioned this in *Persecution and the Art of Writing*. It lies at the heart of John Paul II's *Fides et Ratio*, and of course also of Aquinas and Augustine.

I like to put the issue this way: Unless one goes to the trouble to think things out, following the light of his reason, he will not be in a position to know whether or not something in revelation is addressed to him. He simply will not have reached the limits of reason, pondered sufficiently those questions that reason in fact does not by itself fully answer. But it is to these questions that revelation is primarily addressed. Revelation is not "irrationality" speaking to reason, but mind speaking to mind, ultimately Person speaking to person. This is why, in practice, the pursuit of an understanding of revelation is also a pursuit of philosophy, indeed often a bettering of philosophy.

Philosophy is not the history of philosophy, a confusion that many academic curricula make. But the history of philosophy indicates the myriad ways the human mind seeks to pose and answer its own questions. Some responses are quite frankly nutty. Others are very dubious, some feasible, others make sense but not wholly so. Nothing less than vision finally satisfies the mind. Revelation poses itself as a possible answer to real issues that the human mind has already sought to solve for itself. Revelation can thus indicate why it is not "irrational" to hold what it poses. It does address itself properly to questions that the human mind has raised and knows it does not answer adequately by itself.

Revelation does not exclude considerations of its historically proposed alternatives, rather it insists on dealing with them. From a philosophical view, it merely maintains that it poses a better answer, something at least plausible, but not understood as certain by human reason without faith. That is the barest of touch between human mind in its weakness as intellect, and intellect as such. Acknowledging that a relation exists between reason and what is revealed is merely an affirmation of the fact that something is not wholly unreasonable, because the question revelation answers is itself something that arises in the only reason we have. The revelational answer still requires faith, but a faith that has the effect of making reason more reasonable because it needs to explain itself and acknowledge its limits. Added to this is the fact that also in revelation are found many truths and virtues that can be arrived at by reason, a fact that itself hints that mind is speaking to mind.

Q. #4): (JT) What do you think is the greatest problem with "the University" and higher education today? How can it be improved?

A. #4): (JVS) The answer I will give you comes out of many years of reading Aristotle's *Ethics*. I do not think I would have answered your question quite this way even a year ago.

First, and this is an aside, I think universities in general are too big. One of the really good things happening in this country is the multiplicity of new and improved smaller colleges. Very few foreign countries, however, have ever allowed our multiplicity of different schools even to happen. Most states insist on total control of higher education. The relation between research institutions, think-tanks, colleges, professional schools, and whether they should be in the same institution, needs rethinking. In several ways, on-line access to knowledge and opinion can subsume and bypass universities. The connection between state-federal money and which schools get what is a long and twisted matter.

The greatest American educational law was the G. I. Bill of Rights after World War II. It provided that the money for education went directly to the student, not to the school. The student was the one who decided which school he would attend. The schools had to appeal to the student. The student was really free. As it is today, the cost of education, camouflaged by taxes, makes state schools almost mandatory for many students. I would like to see the choice and will of students and parents always to stand between the school, the teachers' unions, and the faculty.

Somehow at bottom and not wholly unrelated, I think home-schooling has something right about it. Indeed, I think students today should attend college with the serious thought in mind that home-schooling their future children is at least an option for which they prepare themselves. There is also much to be learned from the modern distributists in this connection, from men like Wendell Berry, Allan Carlson, and E. F. Schumacher. But these are opinions.

Aristotle, to return to my main point, asks the question about the relation between one's moral life and one's intellectual life. He is remarkably perceptive. Colleges and universities, as they appear today, usually confront the moral environment of their students not as personal ones, but as some sort of social problems, even social science. The reform of the world, if it needs it, is thus held first to be accomplished at the political level. All sorts of ideologies are imposed on student living, things that affect the student's inner freedom and capacity to know. Things are wrong in the world, it is said, because they are not "structured" correctly. Therefore, change the structures. All will be well. Go to law school. Get into politics. Do service. Rousseau has replaced Plato, but not for the better.

This position looks very nice, I suppose, but if we look at Western nations, including segments of our own, the most striking thing about them is the rapid decline in population and their replacement by peoples from different areas who actually have children and youth. Nothing, including no theory, is changing our world faster than this. We seem blind to it. I suspect, in this regard, that I voice a minority opinion, that Paul VI's much maligned encyclical, *Humanae Vitae,* may well turn out to be the most prophetic document of the last half of the twentieth century. The people who rejected it are rapidly disappearing in our very midst. Already the Grand Tour of Europe is not quite a tour of Europe. Indeed, Europe itself denies much of its own culture. We have forgotten to read Christopher Dawson, who was once at Harvard.

This situation is an aspect of the proper understanding of what is the family, something our own Constitution neglected. But not merely is the family the best and proper place in which to beget and raise children, but the family—husband, wife, and children—is the basic unit of human happiness such as we have it in this world. I know of no better two books on these topics than Jennifer Roback Morse's *Love and Economics* and *Smart Sex: Finding Life-Long Love in a Hook-Up World*. The latter title is a bit flashy, if not fleshy, but it is a book that gets to the heart of the issue, beginning with college life.

And what is that heart? The question as asked has to do with "improving" higher education. My answer is that nothing will really much improve higher education until the question of virtue and its relation to truth is frankly faced. The task of the university is truth, not directly virtue, but the former is not possible without the latter. And by virtue I mean at bottom the moral virtues as described by Aristotle, with the Christian caveat that the problem with virtue is not knowing what the various virtues are— the pagans certainly knew what they are—but, as Augustine said, the problem is the practice or keeping of them. My suspicion is, take it or leave it, that the intellectual disorders of the modern world, within the university and in most individual souls, are almost invariably rooted in moral disorders. There is a very intelligible reason for this connection.

I do not suggest that moral disorders in the souls of individual students somehow lessen IQs or SAT scores. I am reminded that Lucifer was one of the most intelligent of the angels, which intelligence, as such, remains even in his Fall. Likewise, little or no difference in raw intelligence is found between the tyrant and the philosopher-king. What is different is the use to which the intelligence is put as a result of what one chooses to define as his happiness or end. In this sense, much modern thought is a brilliant, ever subtle attempt to justify deviations from the good that is virtue. And once the deviation is accepted, when it is chosen as a way of life, the will to live according to it follows.

In this sense, intellect now becomes a faculty encumbered by one's own chosen disordered passions. It becomes itself an instrument constantly at work giving reasons, both in private and in public, for what is, in effect, a disordered life. I suspect that until this connection of mind and virtue is again recognized, the university, in the sense of the mission to pursue truth as the affirmation of *what is*, will be constantly deflected to the mission of justifying what is in effect a disordered life and, following Plato, a disordered society. Aristotle remarkably said that if we are brought up with good habits, we will not have to worry about understanding first principles when we are old enough to know them because we are already habituated to understanding them, to what is good.

Q. #5): (JT) While teachers are an essential part of successful learning, at the end of the day, much of the responsibility for our education falls on our own shoulders. In your work, you talk about "another sort of learning," and the search for the "higher things." What do you mean by that? What do students have to do to pursue the "higher things?"

A. #5): (JVS) In some sense, this question follows on the previous one. In his wonderful, not-to-be-missed book, *A Guide for the Perplexed*, E. F. Schumacher has a moving description of his own experience on arriving as a young man at Oxford, the great center of learning. By all objective standards, he was where he should have been. He was a very bright young German in the best of the English universities.

Yet, his soul was torn and empty. What he was encountering was utterly unsatisfactory. It was also the product of the great professors. Indeed, that was the problem. His soul was empty. None of the great personal questions that move the human soul was really addressed because the methods proposed for study, in principle, prevented them from being seriously asked.

So what do students have to do to pursue the "highest things"? The first thing they need to do is examine their own souls. I recall a number of years ago, I do not remember where, I found myself chatting with a young Harvard student. Bemusedly, I recalled to him the passage in the *Closing of the American Mind,* in which Bloom quipped that the most unhappy souls in this country are those of the students in the twenty or thirty best and most expensive universities. The young man solemnly told me that he "was not unhappy." All I could do, of course, was laugh.

But Bloom's point was the same as that of Schumacher. Really perceptive students knew that their souls were empty precisely because the logic and methods of what they were learning led to skepticism and meaninglessness. By every objective standard, by an act of faith, that is, they were among the brightest and the best and in the right place, but it wasn't working. It is like the cartoon I once saw in the *New Yorker*, of a group of aging Buddhist monks in a barren monastery. All were sitting on the cold floor in meditative posture, when one very grizzled monk looks up and mutters: "Is this all there is?" I suspect something like this still analogously happens in our universities and to their best students.

If someone is perfectly content with his life and what he is being taught, there is not the slightest possibility that he will ever wonder about its inadequacy. This is why, I think, there must always be a large element of "private initiative" in our own education. I think, in a way, that one can find the basic tools for life—the reading, writing, arithmetic—in almost any school. If one has learned how to read, he has a possibility to be free to educate himself in the highest things against the ideologies that often, knowingly or not, storm through modern universities. Ironically, universities today are criticized for nothing so much as being totally one-sided politically and for their almost universal conformity to a secular view of the world and a corresponding view of human life as itself having no inherent order other than whatever we will.

Mind you, there is nothing wrong with knowing both that something is wrong and in what this wrongness consists. In fact, we are supposed to know not only the truth, but the arguments that can be leveled against it. The highest things are the living a life of virtue that itself points to and accomplishes a life of truth, a knowledge of the truth of things. This involves reason, moderation, and a consideration of revelation. But in addition, both reason and revelation point back to the fact that we live among others and in fact the highest things include others. The contemplative life both presupposes and leads to the realities of our world. Benedict XVI's first encyclical, about active, personal charity, directly recalls that we also encounter the highest things in a love of God that includes the love of our neighbor. This latter emphasis seems to have been one of those things that revelation added to reason.

Q. #60: (JT) College students understand that great grades and test scores were an important reason why they had the opportunity to continue learning in a university. In this world that values measurable performance in the form of GPAs, LSATs, and "resume building," how should Christians, who ought to value more enduring qualities, contextualize such metrics?

A. #6): (JVS) Your phrase "contextualize such metrics" amuses me. I fortunately grew up in an era when such things as GPA, SAT, LSAT, and what all were not yet invented. We did, I believe, have some sort of IQ test administered out of the State of Iowa. I remember being somewhat relieved to learn I was not an idiot, as I think some of my classmates with reason suspected. But this pervasive quantification of criteria is a function of equality theory. Even the slightest preference has to be justified, and the only justification permitted is one based on numbers. This criterion means that courses have to be conceived and taught as if intelligence is capable of being so rendered.

What is not capable of being measured in this way, then, is said not to be intelligence. The whole directly intuitive side of reason is suddenly eliminated. Intelligence is claimed to be only what is measured by these systems, not by *what is*. And since everyone is in institutions because of these tests, it looks like the value of the system is proved when those who are selected are the very ones who reap its rewards by having license to enter the system.

How do Christian students "who ought to value more enduring qualities" cope with such numbers which are in fact the only ticket that will let them into institutions of higher learning? One might say initially that one's Christian values will not in all likelihood be promoted in institutions whose criteria are measured in this way. So again, Christians must be prepared to use their own enterprise and intelligence to encounter what is lacking. To fight for the truth is not all bad.

I have been struck in recent years by what I detect to be an overload in student academic life. To put it in its most succinct terms, students have no time really to learn anything. They are busy, as you say, with "great grades and test scores." Every moment of the day, they are filling up their resumes. They are doing what they think is required to get on, once the university life is over.

There is a remarkable passage in book seven of the *Republic* about the dangers of being exposed to the higher things too soon. Both Plato and

Aristotle give us little grounds for thinking that once we have finished college at twenty-two or so we will have learned much that is really important. Not only are we too young for politics, as Aristotle tells us, but we are too young for philosophy.

We thus lack experience of virtue and vice, or perhaps, in view of my earlier observation, all we have is a world initially seen through our own disorders. We have not read widely enough in literature to understand virtue and vice in others. Indeed, we no longer see the books that call vice "vice" and virtue "virtue," to see what happens to both. And yet Socrates spent his whole life seeking out the potential philosophers. The Christian experience adds repentance to the mix, just as Plato suggested that we should wish to be punished for our own faults and crimes precisely to acknowledge that the norm that we broke was, nonetheless, the correct one for human virtue.

Q. #7: (JT) Christians today might believe that they don't have much use for non-Christian ideas, both from today and from the ages.

A. #7: (JVS) One probably needs to distinguish somewhat between dealing with ideas with no intellectual background available to one and dealing with ideas when one is familiar with them. The phenomenon of *The DaVinci Code*, as I understand it, depends on a massive popular ignorance in the simplest of historical facts and theological concepts, even common sense. However, in principle, ideas from whatever source are to be taken seriously, yet neither naively nor innocently nor uncritically. The famous phrase of Richard Weaver, "ideas have consequences," contains a basic truth—both good and bad ideas have consequences. The origin of almost any political, religious, or cultural change is in the brain of some thinker, usually occurring long before the idea ever reaches the arena of active life.

The contemplative intellectual life is of vital importance both in the Church and in society. Ideas need to be examined, analyzed, criticized, and yes, often combated. Aristotle's "small error in the beginning leads to a large error in the end" is painfully true. But so is the truth that great things begin in hidden, obscure places, like Nazareth. The great wars are first in the minds of what I like to call the "dons," intellectual and clerical. Religious orders in the Church were once designed, in part, to meet this need. But in principle, never neglect the fact that a truly "intellectual life," to use the title of A. D. Sertillanges' famous book, is a much needed and worthy one,

one that honestly and honorably pursues the truth for its own sake. Each of us should have something of this pursuit in our own lives, whatever our particular vocation turns out to be. Plato and Aristotle, Augustine and Aquinas can still be our models.

Q. #8): (JT) In your book, *On the Unseriousness of Human Affairs*, you said that an "academic experience at its highest level requires spiritual vision." Why is that the case? And before we wrap up, what are a few books that you would recommend to students who have a budding interest in Christianity and some books you would recommend to students who are already Christian?

A. #8): (JVS) Perhaps I should say, "academic experience at its highest level leads to spiritual vision." From personal, literary, and anecdotal evidence, my "vision" estimates of folks in academia is modest. But St. Ignatius' principle that we should find God in all things keeps us from forgetting that this vision is also to be found in our daily lives, in those we know and love, in finding the truth of things wherever things are found. Ultimately, any given thing can lead us to all things. Likewise, the understanding of what is the origin of all things takes us back to particular existing things.

With regard to what to read, as you know, advice on what to read has long been a theme of mine. My books, *Another Sort of Learning, A Student's Guide to Liberal Learning,* and *The Unseriousness of Human Affairs,* have in various ways addressed this topic. Each of these books contains various lists of books that touch, in one way or another, on the issue of what and why to read. *Another Sort of Learning* has a very long sub-title that I am rather inordinately fond of, but the short sub-title that I give to it is "how to get an education even while in college."

Though I do not concentrate on them in these books, I am obviously not unconcerned with what are called the classical books. I am always most delighted to spend a whole semester with a class when we read together only Plato, Aristotle, Augustine, or Aquinas. Life is not long enough to do any one of them justice, but a semester is long enough to open our eyes and be astonished. And I am a great believer in C. S. Lewis's admonition that you have not read a great book at all if you have only read it once. He says somewhere that when you have read it thirty or forty times, you will still learn something new. He is right, I think.

I have two other books that will be out shortly on these topics, *The Sum Total of Human Happiness,* by St. Augustine's Press, and *The Life of the Mind,* by ISI Books. First, I begin by recommending certain authors that one should read. Everyone should have and read Boswell's *The Life of Samuel Johnson.* Pascal is not to be missed, nor C. S. Lewis. Chesterton and Josef Pieper should be collected and read again and again. Nothing better will be found. I love Belloc's *The Path to Rome* and *Four Men.* Belloc's essays are as good as essays can be, which is very good. Likewise, his book, *The Crusades,* will be more instructive about what and why things are happening in today's world than almost anything written in the daily papers.

Recently, I have finished Robert Sokolowski's *Christian Faith & Human Understanding.* This is a basic book, not to be missed. His *God of Faith and Reason, Eucharistic Presence,* and *Introduction to Phenomenology* are of major insight and importance.

In 1936, at the school's 300ᵗʰ anniversary, the William James Lecture at Harvard was given by Etienne Gilson under the title, *The Unity of Philosophical Experience.* This book is as fresh and as important today as when it was written. It is simply a must, as are, for those with scientific interests, William Wallace's *Modeling of Nature: The Nature of Science and the Science of Nature,* and Stanley Jaki's *The Road of Science and the Ways to God.* I am also fond of Dennis Quinn's *Iris Exiled: A Synoptic History of Wonder.*

No one should miss Peter Kreeft. I particularly recommend Gertrude von le Fort's *Eternal Woman* and Leon Kass's *The Hungry Soul: Eating and the Perfection of Our Nature,* along with Hadley Arkes's *First Things.* Charles Schulz's *Peanuts* is great. Flannery O'Connor's letters, *The Habit of Being,* are as illuminating a book as one will find. John Paul II's *Crossing the Threshold of Hope* and Benedict XVI's *Salt of the Earth* and *The Spirit of the Liturgy* are mind-openers.

Three books to start with are *Josef Pieper—an Anthology,* Peter Kreeft, *The Philosophy of Tolkien,* and Ralph McInerny, *The Very Spiritual Hours of Jacques Maritain.*

There are the three "after" books, as I call them, each rather heady: Alasdair MacIntyre's *After Virtue,* David Walsh's *After Ideology,* and Catherine Pickstock's *After Writing.* Hans Urs von Balthasar is always good, as is Eric Mascall. Henri de Lubac is very basic. I just came across a little book of Jean Daniélou, *La crise actuelle de l'intelligence,* which I have found very insightful. I have always liked Daniélou's *The Salvation of the Nations*. I do not see why anyone should miss reading Wendell Berry's novels or Waugh's *Brideshead Revisited*, or Sigrid Undset, or Mauriac. The more Newman you have the better.

One must build his own lifetime library—in which he should have the basic works of Plato, Aristotle, Augustine, Aquinas, and the rest, along with the Bible, a good commentary like the *Jerome Biblical Commentary*, and some Fathers of the Church, especially Irenaeus. Books are to be marked, kept, and cherished. A subscription to *L'Osservatore Romano* in English, *Crisis*, *First Things,* and *Catholic World Report*, among others, would not hurt. The website—www.catholidworldreport.com—is good.

Well, even though I have left out too much, this is probably enough for here. Check the above books on learning if you can stand more.

Q. #9): (JT) One last question. What do you think are the most important things we all must study before leaving college?

A. #9): (JVS) The most important thing that you all must learn before leaving college is that you must leave college. College is a privileged place. It was once a place, called by Plato "the Academy," to which knowledge fled when it could not live in the city. It may yet be a place from which one has to flee to know the truth. The most important thing that you must learn is that you may not find the most important things in college. Then again, you may, at least some of them.

I suppose the better question is: "What are the most important things we must study after leaving college?" But this is the same question, in a way. Plato said in the *Laws* and also in the *Republic* that human life is not particularly "important" or "serious." What we must learn is: Why did he say this? He said it because he understood that our delight is in beholding what is really serious, that is, God. Our existence comes to us not by chance or by necessity, but as a gift and as a project. Aquinas said that *homo proprie non humanus sed superhumanus est*, and Augustine explained that, because of this, we have "restless hearts," which we do, in case you have not noticed. But really, the most important thing you must study before you leave college is at least one novel of P. G. Wodehouse. I suggest *Leave It to Psmith* or *Eggs, Beans, and Crumpets*. Why? Because you must see at least one perfect thing in this world, so that you will finally recognize what it is all about when you finally encounter it. This is called the "analogy of being" in metaphysics.

No, on second thought, the one thing you must study before you leave college is the answer to the question that Walker Percy asked in *Lost in the Cosmos*: "Why is it possible to learn more in ten minutes about the Crab Nebula in Taurus, which is 6,000 light-years away, than you presently know about yourself, even though you've been stuck with yourself all your life?"

Stop: the one thing you must learn before leaving college is why Chesterton said at the end of *Orthodoxy* (which, I think, is still the greatest book of the twentieth century) that the one thing Christ concealed from us while He was on earth was His "mirth."

Chapter 2

"It is perhaps not unexpected that a Catholic would see enormous philosophical and theological overtones in the very notion that supper together leads to the highest things."

Interview by Maxwell Woods (MW) with James V. Schall, S.J. (JVS) in *Telos* Magazine.*

Question #1): (MW) Looking back at the essays that you wrote in *Telos*, how did these affect your intellectual understanding?

Answer #1): (JVS) *Telos* is a different and unique forum. It is highly unlikely that mainline academic journals would be free enough to publish a series of what I hope are sensible considerations coming from political philosophy and the Roman Catholic philosophical tradition addressed to mind as such. In this sense, *Telos* does what academic scholarship does not do, namely provide a forum in which the question of revelation is taken seriously and as something directed to reason. The issues that the *Telos* writers are interested in, the proper structure of economics and society, the dangers of totalitarian control, and the intellectual background of ideology are core issues. They almost always have theological origins which cannot be seen without openness to what revelation and the realist philosophy to which it is directed can be frankly considered.

Q. #2): (MW) How does *Telos* fit in with your intellectual world?

A. #2): (JVS) Obviously the very title of the journal—*Telos*—relates to a tradition from at least Aristotle and the Old Testament, to the fact that there are ends in nature and human things that were not eliminated by a modernity that thought it had rejected Aristotle by rejecting any notion of ends in nature. Henry Veatch in his fine book, *Aristotle*, had pointed out

*   *Telos Magazine*, September 1, 2012.

that if the modern explanation of nature was built on a rejection of Aristotle, must we not return to Aristotle when we find the inadequacies of a modernity that now discovers ends all over the place? Teleology was rejected only to come back with more credibility than it ever had before.

My basic approach to the reason and revelation question is first to take care not to make reason a substitute for revelation and, at the same time, not to make revelation an irrational mysticism or voluntarism in which nothing can be related to anything. Revelation is itself reason directed to human reason. And human reason is reason, but not divine reason. Ultimately, there are not two separate sources of reason in the universe. There are beings that reason or have reason in such a fashion that they all share a common origin. In my book *The Modern Age*, I pointed out that the "reason" found in revelation is a more plausible home for man than the constructs of ideological reason designed to replace it.

Reason does not contradict revelation and vice versa. The refusal to address oneself to the claims of reason that flow from revelation is itself irrational. None of this bypasses the difficult intellectual work of seeing the "reasonableness" contained in revelation, nor recognizing the way in which, reasoning about the contents of revelation, we become better philosophers qua philosophers. The real question is why, granted that there are truths beyond reason that the same revelation contains truths that can be verified by reason. I would conclude from this that what is "beyond reason" is not irrational but a rationality of a higher order. When thought about, it makes sense in terms of any proposed alternatives.

Q. #3): (MW) Has there been any significant change since publishing in *Telos?*

A. #3): (JVS) Somehow, rather unexpectedly, I found the editors of *Telos* to be ready to look at an essay on the work of Benedict XVI, who is certainly one of the very greatest minds of our time, and not think themselves odd or unintellectual for publishing it. I have written that Plato's *Gorgias* has many insights that are in line with Roman Catholic thought. The reading of Plato, of course, has long been the locus of consideration of what reason is and what the divine is.

Political philosophy, moreover, has long shown a remarkable affinity for having to include in its considerations both the earthly city and the City of God. The exact location or nature of this latter city has been in our minds at least since Augustine addressed the city that we found in the *Republic* of Plato. Aristotle called politics the highest of the practical sciences. Consideration of any city includes not only its economic and political structures but what is beyond it. Politics points to leisure and to its activities which have to do with the highest things, the things that are not simply political. Political philosophy has in fact been more the locus of the consideration of all disciplines than any other science, often including philosophy itself. The question *quid sit Deus*, as Strauss pointed out, is one that cannot help but arise from a serious consideration of the human things found in political life of any time or place.

Q. #4): (MW) What personalities at *Telos* did you relate with?

A. #4): (JVS) Unfortunately, I have been able to make only one *Telos* January Conference, which quite impressed me. I have found Russell Berman's work to be extremely insightful. I have admired the way Mary Piccone has solidified the work of her husband. Indeed, *Telos*, because of Mary, may be the only journal in the world that enjoys the feast of intellect and a feast of famous Abruzzi dining at the same time. What other journal has a publisher who has produced a first class book on Italian dining! It makes me think of Leon Kass's remarkable book, *The Hungry Soul: Eating and the Perfection of Our Nature*, in which he points out that the highest natural act of our kind is dining together with good friends, good food, good wine, and good conversation about the *things that are*. It is perhaps not unexpected that a Catholic would see enormous philosophical and theological overtones in the very notion that supper together leads to the highest things.

Chapter 3

"And we exist to discover precisely what is serious, which is not ourselves or our works, but God. If we do not include the latter in the adventure of our free lives, we never can complete what they are. We are not, in other words, serious."

Interview by Kathryn Lopez (KL) with James V. Schall, S.J. (JVS)*

Question #1): (KL) How is "retirement"? Will you feel a kinship with Pope Benedict XVI come Thursday?

Answer #1): (JVS) Retirement is a funny word, isn't it? You "withdraw" from something, but it is not life, though it is a phase of life. As I have mentioned elsewhere, I am about six months younger than Pope Benedict, but I announced my retirement six months before he did. Actually, I gave pretty much the same reasons he did, except the "burden" of our respective offices cannot be at all compared. When this Benedict talks of "retirement," however, it means very little in a way. He is a man of mind. Mind remains the same waiting to be thought, be it that of Plato, Aquinas, Samuel Johnson, or Chesterton. Few in the world have really been willing to come to terms with the reordering of mind that this man has accomplished in his long and fruitful lifetime. It is in this reordering that the real seeds of our future lie.

Q.# 2): (KL) How do you think history will remember Pope Benedict XVI?

A. #2): (JVS) It will remember him as the greatest and most learned intellect ever to occupy the Chair of Peter. No public official in our time has been anywhere near his intellectual equal. This disparity is itself the cause of much disorder if we grant, as we must, that truth is the essence of intellect and indeed order. In reading Benedict, I have always been struck

---

* *National Review* on-line, February 26, 2013.

by how familiar he is not just with the Old and New Testaments (in their original languages), but with his constant referring to the Fathers of the Church, especially Augustine, and the intellectual popes like Gregory the Great and Leo the Great, but also Irenaeus, Basil, Maximius, Origen, Bonaventure, and I do not know whom all. He knows German philosophy well, and always cites Plato. He is at home with all the Marxist philosophers. Indeed, in *Spe Salvi*, he cited two of the most famous ones as witness to the logical need of a resurrection of the body. Benedict is a member of one of the French Academies. No one has really begun to do his homework on what this Pope has thought his way through. The media and most universities are, basically, hopeless. I suspect his final *Opera Omnia* in a critical German edition will equal in length that of Augustine, Aquinas, and Bonaventure.

Q. #3): (KL) Why is his *Jesus of Nazareth* significant?

A. #3): (JVS The three volumes of this book should not put us off either because of its length or its erudition. First, the Pope wrote much of this book and published it while he was Pope, but, as it were, not as Pope. That is, it is not an "official" document of the Magisterium. What it is rather is an account of what the man who sits on the Chair of Peter frankly thinks about the key question, "Just who was this Jesus of Nazareth anyhow?" The Pope judged that this mode of identifying himself before the world was a way suitable to our culture. We were asked simply, about Christ, what is the evidence on which you base your acceptance of His Divinity. The book clearly and forcefully lays it out. We can take it or leave it, but not without a nagging sense that we really have not looked at the evidence.

What Benedict did was to state, in brief, his considered opinion and research. He concluded that all the evidence available to us over a two-thousand-year period, including the latest scientific evidence, indicates that Jesus Christ is Who He said He was. That is, He was in fact the Son of God, sent into the world by the Father for the redemption of mankind from their sins. Benedict proceeds to examine all the evidence that this position is not true. Tome after tome have been written to try to prove that Christ never existed, that He was merely a man, that He was a political fanatic, that He was a prophet, that He was a spirit, that He was almost anything but Who and what He said He was. Yet, once one's evidence is set down, it can be examined for its coherence and logic. This examination is what Benedict (and others) has done. If some evidence that makes sense can be shown to disprove the fact, well and good. But it has not been produced yet. In fact, the evidence tends in the direction that the Church has always said it did.

Thus, *Jesus of Nazareth* stands there before us. We may want to do our best to ignore it, as we do not like what it portends if it is true. But if it is true, and the evidence that it is seems to be there, then we can no longer simply go about our business as if something momentous did not happen. If the Word was made flesh and did dwell amongst us, we want to know it, acknowledge it does make a difference to our lives, how we live, how we think.

Q. #4): (KL) What do you mean when you say, as you did in a recent reflection on Pope Benedict and his surprising news that "We are about producing a death, life, hell, and purgatory in this world considerably worse than the worst Christian descriptions of the four last things?" In what way do we do such things? Why would we ever do such things?

A. #4): (JVS) This is but a summary of the Pope's greatest encyclical, *Spe Salvi,* and also of his book *Death and Eternal Life*, among a thousand other places. I have tried to spell it out in my book, *The Modern Age.* Basically, the modern world is an attempt to achieve what are in effect Christian purposes but by rejecting the means of reason and grace that are in fact necessary to achieve them. We now propose an inner-worldly immortality as a goal of science. This is what is behind much medicine and efforts to lengthen human life. We want to "save the earth" so that we can live on it as long as possible. We end up with a new hell on earth. We postpone death and deny birth. But we live on and on. Death is both a liberation and a punishment. If we never die, we are condemned to a useless, ongoing life in this world that is meaningless. The reason we "should ever do such things" is because we deny our transcendent purpose. Once we do this, we have to reinvent ourselves.

This is what has happened in the modern era. One ideology or movement or explanation followed logically from the previous one when it proved untenable. We make past generations to be tools of some utopian vision down the ages in which none of us will appear. But if we understand that each of us is himself created with a personal destiny to live with God, if we choose, we see the world put back in a place of order where it is in effect an arena wherein this ultimate choice for each one of us is played out. We do such things because logically we must, once we insist that there is no transcendent order or that our actions are themselves not judged according to a standard which we do not ourselves create. Our hearts become doubly "restless," to use Augustine's phrase, when we have only ourselves in the cosmos. It is a despair, not a hope.

Q. #5): (KL) Is most of what we occupy ourselves with as a culture and often as a personal matter unserious?

A. #5): (JVS) This question is a compact one. You refer to the title of my book *On the Unseriousness of Human Affairs*. This title comes from Plato who said in his *Laws* that there is only one "serious" thing in the universe and that is God or the Good. All else by comparison is "unserious." That does not mean it is nothing, only that it is not the most important thing about us or the cosmos.

Likewise, your question refers to the classical notion of leisure, to the question, as I like to ask it, "What do we 'do' when all else is done?" As Pieper pointed out in his famous book, the Greek word for leisure, *skole*, is the origin of our word for school. The denial of leisure becomes the classical word for "business," both in Greek and Latin. Thus, the time we devote to keeping alive, to making a living, while necessary and important, is not primarily time "for its own sake." This latter time, as it were, is the time beyond business. It is in this latter time that we should be "free" to think of the highest things. Not to have such time is to be a kind of slave to this world.

Christianity added the notion that all men, whatever their worldly condition, even that of slavery, could reach the highest things through belief and works. In a sense, this is but a perfection of the Greek notion. So when we say that we are "unserious" this is a compliment if understood correctly. We tend to say that something is "useless" or "unserious" to mean that it is not worth much. But in another way, the best thing about us is that we are "useless" or "unserious," that is, we need not exist but we do. And we exist to discover precisely what is serious, which is not ourselves or our works, but God. If we do not include the latter in the adventure of our free lives, we never can complete what they are. We are not, in other words, serious.

Q. #6): (KL) In your *Another Sort of Learning*, you write that: "Anyone with some diligence and some good fortune can find his way to the highest things." How?

A. #6): (JVS) This book arose out of an experience of my own as a young man in the army. I was eighteen years old, had a semester in college, and time on my hands in the barracks. I recall going into the post library one day, looking over the stacks of books, only suddenly to realize that I did not know what to read. In later years, I became aware that it was quite possible to go to college, even have a doctorate, and still have read nothing of real transcendent significance. Eventually, as I learned some of this myself, I realized that a book is a key to many things, especially to some understanding of what it is all about.

So I began to make lists of books, not just any books, but those that, as I like to put it, "tell the truth," those that "turn us around." Initially, these are not the so-called classics. As Leo Strauss said, the great writers contradict each other, and reading great books is more likely to produce skeptics. So the book is a guide through books that have this effect on us. We can be overwhelmed by erudition or scholarship, but it all may be dubious unless we have some kind of sense of metaphysics that enables us to judge about reality. Often the beginnings of wisdom are made too complicated. Yet, I think every mind is capable of knowing and knowing the truth. Every person must find a guide that takes him to the truth. These guides may not live in our lifetime. The trouble with most young men and women is that they do not know where to turn to straighten out their minds about reality. The first step is the Platonic step, the one that causes us to turn around and wonder about something we never encountered before.

Q. #7: (KL) Why is friendship so important?

A. #7: (JVS) In practice, for most of us, its presence in our lives comes close to defining our happiness or lack of it. This is the great theme we find already in Plato and Aristotle. Indeed it is doubtful if anyone has explained to us what friendship is better than these two. All else is a commentary on them or an explanation of the same experience they explained. In one sense, friendship is what college life is about, both understanding what it is, what is means to betray it, what it means ultimately. It is the greatest of our external goods.

Yet, we must be worthy of it. A culture of self-sufficiency makes friendship almost impossible if it is combined with a theory of relativism and denial of virtue. But this is also the topic that takes us to the highest things more quickly than anything else. Aristotle wondered if God was lonely as he did not seem to have any friends. When Christian revelation came to address this topic, we are astonished to read that Christ says to His apostles, "I no longer call you servants but friends." Behind this affirmation stands the Trinity, the teaching of the inner life of the Godhead as containing an otherness that makes it both social and sufficient to itself in a manner that it does not "need" the world. In fact, that is precisely the reason the world itself is not necessary, but the product of gift and freedom.

Q. #8): (KL) What do you think of the New Evangelization?

A. #8): (JVS) Initially, the "new" evangelization was to be directed at the older evangelized countries that have lost much of their faith and accepted many of the most obvious disorders of soul in their polities. Evangelization presupposes a situation that really does not much exist in the world today. A large part of the world, perhaps two-thirds of it, has put up such strong political barriers to anything that might be called a free and honest presentation of Christianity that it is almost impossible to say anything. The Muslim countries, the Chinese, parts of India make it almost impossible to do anything but keep slim contact with Christians who are still allowed to exist. And in the West itself, the ever-increasing barriers caused by "hate speech" and anti-proselytizing legislation, not to mention the increasingly broad definition of secularism which becomes itself a religion of sorts, make the issue rather moot. On the other hand, the essence of the Church is to make known a proper understanding of the world, man, and God, without which men will not properly understand either themselves or the meaning of the world they are given. The electronic world, insofar as it is free, seems able to transcend boundaries, but modern polities still can pretty much control what is allowed to be presented to their population.

Q. #9): (KL) What book of yours do you wish you could share with every person in the world?

A. #9): (JVS) Now that is a question! As far as I know, every book written by anybody is intended for the world. No writer knows who, if anyone, will ever read what he writes. The authors of few books have the slightest idea of who reads his writing. Moreover, many of the writers of books are already long dead, yet their books are still read. The book contains ideas that transcend time. Books, on the other hand, are there, sitting there or on-line, and waiting be read.

But I think that it is safe to say that I, like any writer, wants all he writes to be read. He should not write anything if he did not. Moreover, something can be found in almost any book, even the lousiest, that teaches us something. Now, on this logic, I am not going to list all the books that I have ever written as ones that I hope "every person in the world" would read. I forget how many billions of books are in the Library of Congress, but I would accord the writer of each of these books the same sense that he wants everyone in the world to read what he wrote. And when you address yourself to the possibility of this happening, considering the vast scope of what is in books, we realize that the very existence of so many books and of their intended readers takes us to an argument for eternal life.

Q. #10): (KL) Save for the Bible, what is the book that everyone needs to read?

A. #10): (JVS) You ask easy questions! Not everyone would list the Bible. I have a new book coming out called *Reading Belloc*. I love the story that someone told me. Belloc, in his old age, there in Kings Land in Sussex, read but three books: P. G. Wodehouse, *The Diary of a Nobody*, and his own works. Yet, I do think that some books are more important than others, provided in another sense that my doubt about whether there is such a thing as an "unimportant" book is not forgotten. I am used to giving short lists of books. In talking to a student or someone by chance, you realize that he has not really read anything important in the sense of bringing him out of himself. Books that do this best, I think, and there are others, are Boswell's *Life of Johnson*, Schumacher's *A Guide for the Perplexed*, Chesterton's *Orthodoxy*, Tolkien's *Lord of the Rings*, and, of course, Plato, Aristotle, Augustine, Aquinas, and Dante. Most folks need some help to begin these things. C. S. Lewis is always a good place to begin. Yet, if you ask me tomorrow, I will have some others.

Q. #11): (KL) Should we read the Bible? How should we read the Bible?

A. #11): (JVS) An advantage of being a priest is that reading some small selection of the Bible is part of his everyday routine. The Bible is a vast work. It is not to be read "as literature," but because it is true. It is amazing how one can read it again and again and always find something that he did not see before. This is true of Plato also, of course. Indeed, a reading of Plato is not a bad way to learn to read the Bible. Basically, we read the Bible to know what it teaches and says. We also read it to learn how to know and worship God. The Bible is a book addressed to our souls. It is not just a tractate or treatise, but an account of God's teaching us what we need to know. Part of what it teaches us, we could figure out by ourselves if we are lucky. But most of it is what we could not know by our own powers. Yet, it is clearly the answer for many of the most basic queries that we have about life—why do I exist? What is my destiny? Why do we suffer? What is the purpose of existence? What about death and sin? Can we be forgiven? How ought I to live?

Q. #12): (KL) Why are you not an advocate of Great Books?

A. #12): (JVS) As Msgr. Sokolowski says, the first step in philosophy is to make "distinctions." We should read books, great and otherwise. The so-called "Great Books Programs" have received much attention and controversy about "What makes a book great?" The Great Books Programs, as I understand them, grew out of a rejection of first-hand philosophical study and examination. Philosophy was replaced by the history of philosophy. They are not the same thing, though there is absolutely nothing wrong with knowing what a famous great book contains, even if you think it idiotic or dangerous.

If you simply read through the ten or twenty Great Books, chances are you will end up skeptics. The Great Books, as Strauss said, contradict each other. One of course must make a coherent effort to see how ideas relate to each other in different thinkers. This "seeing" is why Gilson's *Unity of Philosophic Experience* or David Walsh's *Modern Philosophical Revolution* is important. But unless we have some sense that we can philosophize and that philosophizing is not just tossing off our own nutty opinions about whatever comes into our heads, as Plato said, we will not be able properly to see why many of the Great Books are great because, as Strauss also said, they contain "brilliant errors." It takes some original philosophizing to know why and how an error can be "brilliant."

Q. #13): (KL) You had websites long before the Pope started Tweeting. Do you worry about the attention spans of your students? Are we ruining our minds? Our ability to think and to write?

A. #13): (JVS) I do not worry so much about the attention spans of my students as about my own! I have never Tweeted in my life. I hope it does not show. My basic view of students is that they are always twenty years old when I see them. They can usually read and write and use all known electronic devices that do everything from taking photos, to looking up baseball statistics, to popping corn. The era of not knowing facts is over. Half the fun of life is gone.

But seriously (or un-seriously, as the case may be), it has been my experience that if you know and give good books to students, if you read along with them, if you are alert to the wonder in them, their minds will become alert. They will "turn around," to use Plato's phrase. This is almost the only transcendent task of a college professor. He cannot "make" a student read. He can require; he can cajole; he can humor; he can urge; but ultimately it must come from within the student himself. He must wake up one morning and say to himself, "I want to know that." When that happens, the professor's task is basically over. From then on, his relation with his students is a pleasure. And as Aristotle said, we must, at the risk of missing it all, experience the pleasures of simply thinking for its own sake, because what we now know is true and we know it.

Q. #14): (KL) Is there anything more that you wish that you could have included in your "last lecture?"

A. #14): (JVS) I asked one of my former students, a perceptive young lady, how long this lecture should be. She responded: "If it is anything longer than forty-five minutes, it had better be a barn-burner." That was good advice. The problem with most lectures and lecturers is that they are too long, not too short. Just what is exactly right is a question of prudence and insight. That being said, I have other lectures, say my "next-to-last" lecture, that would touch on tyranny, or the order of the cosmos, or what is medieval political philosophy? The "last lecture" was requested by students and it seemed proper to me to do as I cited from Frederick Wilhelmsen that a professor is not a professor if he does not state in his notes or writing or lecture what he holds, what he thinks is true. Students who have had me in several classes over the years know what I have to say. When one comes to his last class, he hopes that he has done what a professor should do, namely, take them to what is true, to what makes sense, to *what is*, as I like to put it.

Q. #15): (KL) For many of us, we no longer have a vocation or sense of reality that enables us by our devotion or meditation to transcend how our politics defines us, as you wrote in *Another Sort of Learning*. Has that only gotten worse? How much do you worry about our hyper-partisanship, and, well, across-the-board hyper-activity?

A. #15): (JVS) I had forgotten that sentence. But certainly it has gotten worse. This is because the political order is no longer limited to politics. With the rejection of revelation and natural law, all that is really left is politics or, as Charles N. R. McCoy used to put it, a "substitute metaphysics." It is an elevation of a mindless action to the center of human life. Human action is a noble thing, as Hannah Arendt said in her great book, but it cannot replace the order of leisure. This is why we have to escape from the in-built philosophical assumptions that are present in the culture itself, as Tracey Rowland put it. I have always been impressed with a comment that Eric Voegelin made in Montreal in 1976, to the effect that "no one needs to participate in the aberrations of his time." Solzhenitsyn found in the Gulag itself a final freedom where they could no longer take anything away from him, namely his real freedom to state the truth. But they can kill him. That is still why the deaths of Socrates and Christ stand at the heart of political philosophy. The state can, and the democratic state seems more and more inclined, to take the direction of killing Socrates and Christ, killing anything that stands in its way of imposing its own order on the souls of men, men too often willing to let it happen.

Q. #16): (KL) What is your advice for always doing the work of telling the truth and waking the world up in a world that isn't always sure that there even is such a thing as truth?

A. #16): (JVS) My initial answer is, "Read Plato!" The next step is to, "Read Aristotle!" We have not transcended Plato and Aristotle. In fact, what we have done is carry out in our lives the trends and aberrations that they described. The best description of the American polity today, at its core, is found in the *Politics* of Aristotle and the *Republic* of Plato when they tell us the sequence of disorder or deviations from the good. As I read them, we follow almost exactly what they saw because they understood the principles at work in a human soul that rejects the good one step at a time.

But I am a follower of Socrates. The reform of all social life begins in the soul of one person, and then another. This is why great things always begin in small, out-of-the-way places. The picture of our society is not pretty. But if we hold to the Socratic principle that no harm can come to a good man, and that we realize that death is not the worst evil, but denying good is, then we shall rest content and "all will be well."

Chapter 4

"The Christian faith does not think that one generation exists so that another generation down the line will be perfect. In that sense, no generation stands closer to God than another."

Interview by Robert Reilly (RR) with James V. Schall, S.J. (JVS) for Inside Catholic.*

Question #1): (RR) What is the most important thing you teach?"

Answer #1): (JVS) One could approach this question several ways: "What is the most important course?" or "What is the most important idea?" or "What is the most important thing that you want students to come away from in your classes having learned?"

For over thirty years now, I have been teaching the same course every semester. Its size ranges from 90-100 or so students. It is called, an old-fashioned title, I suppose, "Elements of Political Theory." The title I inherited from the department. In my mind, it is a political philosophy course in the broadest sense of that word. To do political philosophy right, you have to include things beyond it like metaphysics and revelation, and things below it, like practical political life, economics. Geography and history come in as do wars and rumors of war. Politics, as Aristotle said, is the highest of the practical sciences, but not the highest science as such. This means that politics is limited by what it is not. Politics does not make man to be man but takes him from nature as already man and guides him to be good, as Aristotle also said.

Still, I suspect the most important thing I assume in teaching is that students be themselves docile, that is, as I like to put it, that they be "eminently teachable." I like the remark of Allan Bloom in *Shakespeare's Politics*: "A man is most what he is as a result of what he does; a man is known, not

---

* Interview with Robert Reilly in *Inside Catholic*, on-line, November 20, 2007.

simply by his existence, but by the character of his actions—liberal or greedy, courageous or cowardly, frank or sly, moderate or profligate" (5). To be teachable means that a student first realizes in his soul that he does not already know too much. Nor is his purpose in learning simply about grades. Aristotle's notion that there are things worth knowing "for their own sakes" strikes me as the most important thing I have to teach.

But it is not enough to say, "Look here, son, you need to know about, say, Dante or Cicero." It is alright to say this to him, of course, and a teacher should say it. Authority means something, gives directions. What needs to happen, however, is that a student sees in his own soul that something both can be learned and is worthy of being known. Indeed, he needs suddenly to rouse himself and find delight in something that he now knows. There is a delight in knowing unlike any other delight, the absence of which, as Aristotle also said, is a very dangerous thing, especially for politicians.

Q. #2): (RR) What is the hardest thing to teach (in the sense of the receptivity of the students to it)?

A. #2): (JVS) One is tempted to say "the truth." Chesterton's famous quip, which I often cite, is pertinent here. "There is no such thing as an uninteresting subject, only uninterested people." Yves Simon has a very insightful section in *A General Theory of Authority* which he entitles "Freedom from the Self." In an age of self and self-expression, this notion that our very selves can be obstacles to our own freedom comes as a shock. Freedom from our very selves? What can this mean? The whole idea of virtue is that we will only see ourselves if we choose a proper end and means to achieve it. The old monks used to speak of "conquering ourselves." They spoke of this inner war of ourselves against ourselves as the most difficult and perhaps dangerous enterprise of all. It is a Platonic idea, to be sure. All disorder of the world originates in disorder of soul. If we do not learn this truth, nothing else will much matter as we are bound to get it wrong because we choose to see things wrongly.

Thus if we do not know we have a soul, if we are just a bundle of emotions and drives, we will never be sufficiently free of ourselves to see what is not ourselves. No freedom is more precious than that of seeing clearly, delightedly, what is not ourselves. We are, as it were, self-insufficient. And that, in a way, is the best thing about us. We look to others to know what we really are. We are not merely coupling and political animals, as Aristotle said, but, as he also said, beings who wonder what it is all about. The beginnings of this wonderment are precious moments in our lives. It often happens through first loves, or through being struck by something we never saw before or even heard of. It can even happen in a university class.

Q. #3): (RR) You have said that the one thing of which you can be sure is that all your incoming students at Georgetown will be relativists. What is there left to appeal to in them?

A. #3): (JVS) Actually, that was a reference to Allan Bloom who applied it to most all incoming students in any university. It is what they learned from the culture. Student relativists are often second-hand ones, however. By that I mean that they have heard this mild skepticism from a sharp teacher in high school, or from watching an intellectual program on PBS, or from being frustrated in their own search for explanations of even the simplest of things. I also suspect that it often has some relation to divorce in the family.

What is there left to appeal to? Much, I think. I am rather fond of that famous remark of C. S. Lewis that the young atheist can never be too careful of what he reads. And this is very true. The really frightening thing for many students is the suspicion that there may well be cogent arguments for the truth of things. They are even more astonished when they begin to suspect that the argument for revelational things has much more to be said for it than anyone ever told them about. We should never forget that twenty-year-old students, like ourselves once, were indeed only twenty years old. Each person has a capacity for the adventure that each soul in its very creation stands for, the adventure of seeking to know what it is all about.

All I really ask a student to bring with him to class is himself, not a computer, not even a pencil. I will read with them what I have myself pondered and read over and over again for many years. I am still astonished by these things. A professor can "make" no student see what is there, but he can call his attention to things that are, in their own ways, remarkably insightful and profound. Often college students are too young yet; twenty is still quite young for intellectual things, as Plato never tires of telling us. We are fools if we think that great things do not mostly require time and growth. Aristotle said that the young are not fit for politics because they lack experience. It is not in politics alone that this condition is present in them. But the whole adventure of being young is that you suspect that you have begun something about whose end you have only the vaguest notion, even when you are fortunate enough to be able to state it in Platonic or revelational terms.

Q. #4): (RR) You often quote Socrates in saying that the worst thing a man can do is to lie in his soul about the good. How deeply embedded is that lie in today's culture from which these students come?

A. #4): (JVS) Yes, to have a lie in our soul about *what is*, this is the very worst thing that can happen to us. No one could put such a lie there but we ourselves. We usually put it there because we want to lie to ourselves in order to continue doing what does not conform to the proper order of our soul. The Socratic phrase is extremely evocative, I think. It is again a theme that we touched on earlier. The ultimate drama has to do with, while remaining ourselves, being called out of ourselves, often through encountering even the most pedestrian things, but more often through the fine things like friendship.

What always makes me realize that it is all worthwhile is that I almost never meet students who do not already in their young lives wonder what friendship is about. The greatest treatments of the topic are still in Aristotle and the Gospel of John. This is, ultimately, the topic, when carefully spelled out, that gets to the very heart of the Trinity, if we are willing to pursue it far enough. No one can avoid attending to the meaning of this experience.

Pope Benedict recently spoke of the degree to which habits and customs in a culture could obscure or even eliminate our awareness of the right order of soul. This recalled Aquinas' question about whether the natural law could be "blotted out" of the human soul. Aquinas thought it could come pretty close, though not entirely.

In speaking of Machiavelli, I always tell the students that there is nothing in Machiavelli, that is, no horrid deed of man, that is not already in Plato, Aristotle, Augustine, and Aquinas. The difference between Machiavelli and Aristotle was not that Machiavelli knew something that Aristotle did not. Machiavelli has obviously gotten many of his most troubling precepts from Aristotle, who knew exactly what a tyrant was and told us so. The difference between them was, of course, that Machiavelli held that it was all right to do what Aristotle held that it was not. The difference was choice, not knowledge.

The point I want to make with regard to your last question about the culture is that, however much customs and habits corrupt, there can always remain a spark of light within individual souls. By virtue of chance reading, a tragedy, political or personal, a love, a sacrifice, one can be awakened to act contrary to the disorder in the culture. We still must at least suspect that more souls were actually saved in a concentration camp than in a university faculty, a television office, a business or government bureaucracy. The latter worlds are not closed off either. However deeply embedded the "lie" is in either our soul or our culture, the adventure of a return to sanity remains possible. In its own way, I suppose, even damnation is an adventure, as stories depicting the devil seem always to remind us. But hopefully they teach us that there are certain adventures on which we do not want to embark.

Q. #5): (RR) Can you inoculate students against this influence? How?

A. #5: (JVS) I suppose, using your metaphor, I do not want to "inoculate" anybody against anything except perhaps the flu. What you mean, of course, is to ask if there is a way for the student to become aware of the inbuilt presuppositions of the culture that affect him almost without his realizing it. Tracey Rowland, in her important book *Thomism and Modern Culture*, has shown that within a culture itself are already operative principles and presuppositions which, it we are not specifically aware of them, will serve to direct our efforts in the way of the habits within the culture. If these habits are disoriented, the person who assumes that the culture is morally neutral will find himself going along with the presuppositions of the culture to his own detriment.

We forget the enormous attraction of "prestige." If it is in an important journal, or on a famous television program, or the normal presuppositions of a famous university, we will assume that this view is where the cutting edge is. But this is surface. In this area, there is no saving of someone who won't be saved. What I try to do, rather, is to introduce students to books and authors who are articulate, intelligent, and persuasive, so that they will begin to see that intelligence is not wholly on the side of disorder of soul. Students, I think, are really crying for some guidance or hint of what else is there. They are astonished to find so much whose existence is not even hinted at. But someone has to give them a start. It does not take much to arouse a suspicion in their minds that they have not heard the whole story. An essay of Chesterton or C. S. Lewis is often enough to provoke interest.

Students also need living examples, though often the greatest teachers have long been dead. There are few places, however, in which there are not one or two teachers who are aware of the problem. Eric Voegelin once remarked that we do not have to participate in the disorders of our time. I think this is true. We may not become famous, but we can hold our own counsel about the meaning of things. Thus, the primary way to "inoculate" is to let them know that there is some other source of persuasive argument and knowledge that is not being honestly presented in the university they attend. Once they at least suspect this deficiency and are exposed to and understand a few books or essays that make sense, common sense, the student is pretty safe, I think.

Q. #6): (RR) How discouraged are you at the degraded level of public discourse in America today? What is the path to recovery? Can it come politically?

A. #6): (JVS) A nation has to live with the choices it makes. We were extremely fortunate that George Bush was president on 9/11, I think. Whether we will be so fortunate the next time, I am not optimistic. The country seemingly will not face the fact that it has an enemy that is often much shrewder and more determined than its own leaders. It is not so much that "public discourse" is degraded, but the moral level of the society itself, particularly as this level is encouraged or reinforced by law.

Nations rise and fall. We are no exception. And the rise and fall usually have rather much to do with the internal moral condition of the souls of the citizens. What we choose to make of ourselves is not immune from external and political consequences. A political recovery is certainly part, though not the most important part of the problem. We look on public decency and morality as an internal or personal problem. It is that, but much more. No fault or sin can fail to have external consequences, no matter how "private." The distinction of public and private is useful and has a real basis in fact.

The "path to recovery" cannot bypass this inner soul issue. We forget that we are not made for this world, even though we are by nature political animals. No public order is anything but transient, even if it has lasted several centuries, as has ours. Modern ideology has tried to convince us that the main thing that we are here for is to form some future utopia down the ages. What is new is perhaps the rise of Islam, which more or less holds the same thing, namely that it seeks to conquer the whole world for Allah. But this latter is so inadequate as both an inner-worldly purpose and a description of transcendent destiny that it borders on the same goals as later ideology.

I sometimes think that above all we need a proper understanding of Heaven. Peter Kreeft has a good book on this topic. In fact, Pete Kreeft has a good book on just about everything worthwhile. We sometimes cannot or will not understand that the most fundamental issues are theological. But they are not just any theology. Modern liberalism wants to tell us that we dare not confront theological issues because it will cause fanaticism and war. One suspects that not confronting them will cause even greater fanaticism and war.

Q. #7): (RR) Do you think America is misrepresented abroad, especially in the Muslim world, or do they see us as we are, a center of unbelief and corruption?

A. #7): (JVS) It is possible that we are both "misrepresented" and that we have considerable "unbelief and corruption." I am inclined to think that if we were totally pious and virtuous we would be even more misrepresented in the Islamic world. It is not our vices that threaten Islam, but our truth, insofar as we acknowledge it ourselves, which is rather rarely the case.

We may be more deliberately misrepresented in a Europe which is slower to recognize threats to itself than we are. Europe is almost blind in its failure to assist those who have guaranteed its own relative freedom. The current crisis of the world, I think, is more fundamentally in Europe than in Islam. Nothing is more astonishing than the decline in population in Europe. Those who know about *Humanae Vitae* are not particularly surprised at this decline which opens Europe to what is in effect, after Tours and Lepanto, a delayed Muslim invasion. This time, the invasion is not primarily military, which is probably why it is so effective.

We who understand the abidingness of the Fall cannot be overly astonished at widespread unbelief and corruption. We have read our Thucydides, our St. Augustine, and our Burke. The temptation of modern Christians, under the name of social justice, is often to forget or reject Augustine's "political realism." The purpose of our presence in this world is not that one generation is sacrificed to another. We are all equally close to the Godhead. Modern liberalism was often constructed as a way to replace original sin. It thought that it could, by its own powers, establish a world without blemish. We who are Christian recognize that the whole point of salvation through Incarnation was that everyone, if he chose in grace, might be saved, no matter what sort of a regime or culture he lived in. Yet we have to acknowledge, on the basis of modern experience, that politics can go a long way in preventing a proper understanding of human destiny from even being considered.

Q. #8): (RR) You are one of the great defenders of the paramount status of reason. Is it accurate to say you insist on the standard of reason in judging the intelligibility of faith?

A. #8): (JVS) It is not so much that Schall insists on the centrality of reason. It is that the faith itself insists on it. We have intellects but we are not gods. The Greeks used to say that the gods do not philosophize, for they are already wise. The purpose of philosophy is that we become wise. What does this mean, to be wise? It means that we seek to know and affirm "the order of things." This latter is the title of a new book of mine, *The Order of Things*.

Our intellects are intellects, but they are not divine or angelic intellects. This limitation means that by our intellects we seek to know *what things are*. What we mean by faith, by *fides quaerens intellectum*, is that faith's own propositions or structure, as it is revealed to us in scripture and tradition, is itself directed to intellect, to our intellects as they are active in seeking to know things *that are*. What we have to be careful of is the idea that somehow because we have intellects, therefore we could figure out the transcendent order all by ourselves. If we could do this we would already be gods.

We do not seek to be gods. It is alright that we are what we are. But what we are is a noble and exalted thing once we realize that God wants us to know Him, both through the intelligibility of creation and through seeking to know Him "face-to-face," something that scripture indicates is in fact our destiny. This seeking suggests that the pursuit of intelligence is not just a pursuit of knowledge but of someone who knows and can be known.

Yet, from our side, we at least need to have grounds provided by reason why any religion or revelation might be credible. If such grounds exist, we must take a further look at what the content of this revelation is. And if we find that somehow, in our pursuit of understanding it, we find ourselves learning more and more about truth and ourselves, we can suspect that there is a relation between this revelation and what we can know by our own powers.

The opposite is the case, as *Fides et Ratio* suggested. Let us suppose, for example, that our own philosophic presuppositions in epistemology, for instance, did not allow us to affirm that Christ really existed as a human being seen and spoken to by other human beings. If such a philosophic position were true, we could not believe that Christ was as He claimed to be, true God and true man. At this juncture, we have a choice, either to deny the very suppositions of the faith narrative or to question the philosophy that prevents us from affirming *what is.*

Q. #9): (RR) By that standard, how do you rate the chances of Islam reconciling itself with reason in the way Aquinas achieved for Christianity? What happens if it does not?

A. #9): (JVS) Actually, to use your phrase, I rate the chances pretty close to zero. Moreover, I consider the project or policy of "secularizing" Islam in the hope of modifying its aggressiveness to be also wrong-headed. Indeed, a good part of Islam, as I understand it, does not think this reconciliation is possible either, if we mean by reason that foundation of philosophic reasoning founded by the Greeks and carried on by subsequent thinkers. Some of these latter were also Muslim, but their views are mostly rejected because they "limit" the "power" of Allah. That is, reason denies even to the Godhead the possibility of affirming the truth of contradictories. Of course, this inability to contradict itself is not really a "limitation" on God, but the very basis of the *Logos* that defines *what He is.*

The classic issue of the so-called "two truths" remains pertinent even as an issue in contemporary politics. In order to save the presumed truths of the Koran, it was proposed that there could be statements of reason and statements of the Koran that contradicted each other, but still could both be true. This view has the effect of dividing the soul of the believer into two parts. What happened is that one group, the philosophers, went one way and the theologians another. Christianity cannot have this problem of conceiving a contradiction between faith and reason. If such a contradiction is true, then clearly Christianity is false, by its own standards.

Q. #10): (RR) Is Islam compatible with anything but itself?

A. #10): (JVS) The real issue that interests us is rather "Is Islam compatible with itself?" This issue is our main problem with Islam and constitutes the heart of the question of the justice of its expansion and the means used to accomplish it. Pope Benedict's question in his Regensburg Lecture was simply, "Is it reasonable to use violence to spread religion?" If the claim is that it is not reasonable, then we are all in agreement. If the claim is that it is reasonable, then we have to find out what understanding of what is "reasonable" could possibly arrive at such a conclusion. The answer is that "reason" is really will. That is, that there really is no such thing as reason.

What we find difficult to understand is that there is an "intellectual" justification for the use of violence in the expansion of religion (or in the attainment of political goals). This justification involves the claim that Allah can do anything including making contradictories compatible. This "making" compatible is not, of course, intellectually tenable, but it is held to be nonetheless. Thus if Allah is pure will, it is possible for him to will the contradictory of what he willed before. He is bound by nothing, including his own rules. To claim otherwise in this view would be to limit the power of Allah. Hence, it is blasphemy to seek to so limit him.

On first hearing this view, we think it absurd. But if we look at the justifications for abortion, they are logically of the same philosophical basis. Namely, there is no binding principle of reason. Whatever is willed by a majority, a court, or a ruler is law. Reason has nothing to do with it. There is, as the Pope implied in the Regensburg Lecture, a not so strange similarity between current Muslim thought and current Western thought.

So logically, Islam is compatible with much modern Western thought, that thought which is based in a voluntarist theory of metaphysics, law, and theology. This similarity probably explains the painful reluctance of Western liberalism to come to terms with the implications of Islam's claim to rule the world. Religious believers, following what they hold to be the "logic" of their faith, are written off as terrorists and fanatics. They will never be understood in these terms, I suspect.

Q. #11): (RR) President Bush (George W. Bush) referred to the current struggle with radical Islam as "ideological." Is that a correct designation?

A. #11): (JVS) I think not, or if so, in a very restrictive sense. The struggle with Islam is theological in nature, not ideological. That is, it is not to be understood primarily in terms of Western philosophy or sociology.

Generally, Western books seek to reduce "terrorism" to some characteristics intelligible in scientific terms. These scientific terms have their own philosophic presuppositions. They omit religion or identify it with ideology. Ideology is the projection onto reality of an idea that has its origin in human confabulation that seeks to explain reality in terms of some *a priori* intelligence.

Islam has not in fact changed much since its beginning. This inner cohesiveness is its strength, if strength it be. If we seek to understand Islam in ideological terms, we will never grasp what is going on. What is going on? We have the resurgence of a relatively ancient faith that now sees or thinks it sees the possibility of overcoming a centuries-old impediment to its expansion. This mandate to world conquest, in its view, is willed by Allah. It depends on constant expansion eventually to include the whole world.

Such is the opportunity that thinkers and actors like Bin Laden see presented them in the internal moral disorder and lack of will in the West. This same West, the so-called "Crusaders," are seen as the enemy. They were the ones that, in some regards miraculously at Tours and Lepanto and Vienna, prevented Islam from conquering Europe much earlier. This obstacle is what must be reversed. The radical Muslim mind sees this revitalized expansion as now possible, with the aid of Western laws and its need for labor in light of its own radically declining birthrate.

Thus, I have often thought that identifying the problem as with ideological terrorists completely misses the boat and prevents Western powers from seeing the real nature of the attacks being made against them. On the other hand, it is in Islam's interest not to provoke actual military expansion too much. It can win on the demographic front if it is patient. Western thinkers conceive "terrorism" to be a kind of ideological construct that can be applied to many societies. Hence Islam, with its theology, is not itself looked upon as the origin of the problem. The uniqueness of Islam itself is overlooked.

Islam is, I think, consistent with itself. We cannot or will not understand this religion because we think that we can analyze Islam in terms of Western thought, which insists that we analyze Islam after the manner of ecumenical or liberal concepts. In this view, understanding of Islam is really an understanding of Western categories, not of Islam itself. This fixation on ideology, then, makes it impossible to see the real enemy and his intentions, which are not ideological but religious. What we refuse to understand is a militant religion and the theology behind it. We fail to give it the "dignity" it deserves on its own terms.

Q. #12): (RR) Is the West equipped to fight this struggle at the level at which it is taking place?

A. #12): (JVS) I do not think so. We do not think that ideas matter. As I have said elsewhere, all wars, including those in the name of religion, begin in the mind, not on the battlefield. The failure of Christianity and Judaism, let alone the other religions and philosophies, to come to terms with the truth claim of Islam and the evidence, if any, on which it is based is where the problem lies. I have often lamented the fact that the Church has never issued an encyclical with the title "What Is Islam?" Islam specifically denies the basic Christian doctrines of Incarnation and Trinity. We do not begrudge them this denial, for that is their position. But the truth status of this denial is not just a question of tolerant discussion with whoever will discuss the issue. I do not think, ultimately, that the truth claim of Islam can be avoided in the name of tolerance or ecumenism. This is where the problem lies.

The liberal notion about the way to deal with Islam is to introduce a doubt into the souls of its believers. This doubt will lower, it is said, religious fanaticism. This approach may work with Christians, but it will not work with Islam. We have never faced up to the question of why Islam is so impossible to convert or deal with. Until this question is faced, discussion of our dealings with Islam will always have a superficial tone to them. One of the obvious signs of lack of "equipment" to "fight" this struggle is that we do not demand a *quid pro quo* with Islam. Islamic emigrants into Western societies quickly learn to use our laws to form themselves into cohesive groups within our societies. These groups do not assimilate; they separate. Religious freedom means setting up one's own system that was brought with him.

Thousands and thousands of mosques are built in every neutral and Western country. No demand is ever forcefully made for reciprocity. When American forces were fighting in the first Gulf War, they were not allowed to have a copy of the Bible, even though we were fighting the Saudi battle for them. Nothing better shows our failure to understand what is at stake than these lost opportunities. Since we cannot or will not grant religious motivation over time, we fail to see what is happening. Otherwise, it is a one-way street that simultaneously prevents any Western presence within Muslim lands and permits Muslim presence in our lands but on its terms, not ours. Our laws can be used not for a Christian but ironically for a Muslim purpose. Muslim laws cannot be used to our advantage. We are the only ones who do not seem to notice this paradox.

Q. #13: (RR) Which of your more than twenty books would you recommend as a place to start reading your thought?

A. #13): (JVS) Without any question, the place to begin reading Schall is with *Another Sort of Learning*. This book sets the agenda. It is a book that takes the reader out of Schall and directs him to the things that count. It asks the crucial question, "What do we do if we suspect that the highest things were not, are not, being presented in our universities or in our culture?" We do not, I think, despair. The later books, *On the Unseriousness of Human Affairs*, *The Life of the Mind*, *A Student's Guide to Liberal Learning*, and *The Sum Total of Human Happiness* follow and deepen the initial inspiration of *Another Sort of Learning*.

In some sense, I follow the admonition of Aquinas when he said that those things we have contemplated in our own souls are to be handed over or passed on to others, the famous *contemplata tradere*, to pass on what one has pondered. My approach is not one through the "Great Books." It is, as it were, the Great Books once removed. I am clearly not hostile to reading the Great Books. But I am aware that they can confuse if they are not read with a previous realist philosophy. The Great Books were in some sense, as Frederick Wilhelmsen once pointed out, invented to substitute for philosophy as an original discipline. My book lists, found in various books, I think, always take the reader back to *what is*.

I might add, however, that I think that many of the best things that I do are in short essay form. I have written hundreds of these essays. I have often said that Belloc is the greatest essayist in the English language. He is, in this sense, a hero of mine. In addition he is a prophet of the rise of Islam in our time. His short essays, in any case, are gems of travel, insight, walking, humor, nostalgia, philosophy, history, and faith. So I am particularly fond of my essay books, *Idylls and Rambles*, *Schall on Chesterton*, *The Praise of "Sons of Bitches,"* and *The Distinctiveness of Christianity*. I have had several series of monthly or quarterly columns over the years: "Sense and Nonsense," "On Letters and Essays," "English Essays," and several others that come and go. It is the challenge of the mind, as Aquinas taught, to state clearly and succinctly *what is*, to articulate what is true. No form does this better than the short essay, I think.

My political philosophy books are in their own ways related to the question of learning and the essay. Political philosophy occupies a special place in the order of knowledge. It takes us by being itself into the realm of theory or contemplation, but it also must know history, economics, theology, the various human disciplines, and science itself. The political philosophy books—*The Politics of Heaven and Hell; Reason, Revelation and the Foundations of Political Philosophy; At the Limits of Political Philosophy; Jacques Maritain: The Philosopher in Society; Roman Catholic Philosophy*; and the *Regensburg Lecture*—all circle around the same fundamental problem: namely, how does reason address intelligence and how does intelligence address reason, and within these questions what is the place and limits of the city?

Finally, it would not be proper to close these reflections on Schall books without a specific mention of Chesterton. He remains the most remarkable of minds. He is common sense, but he is also a metaphysician. He is at home everywhere. It is this breadth, coupled with humor and logic, that reassures us that the philosophers are not really the last word. I have read few paragraphs in Chesterton that did not lead me from something to everything. He is almost uncanny. That is, he knows *what is*.

Q. #14): (RR) You have frequently remarked that Catholicism has never been intellectually stronger and culturally weaker. Why do you maintain this?

A. #14): (JVS) I am a great admirer of the work of Msgr. Robert Sokolowski. His essay on the understanding of the Eucharist in his *Christian Faith & Human Understanding* is a remarkable analysis of the human mind doing everything it can to prevent itself from understanding or admitting the truth of the Eucharist. Our time is remarkable in the fact that often the most brilliant public leaders are found on the See of Peter. Catholicism, as I often say, addresses itself to intellect and does not hesitate to do so.

Yet, as Tracey Rowland, whom I mentioned previously, pointed out, for all the perceptiveness of Church leaders, they often did not realize the way a culture comes to embody principles of disorder or immorality that are found in the very laws and practices of a culture. In thinking that the mission of the Church was to "open itself to modern culture," we found ourselves accepting ways of thought and life that were incompatible with what the faith understood God and human destiny to be about. The general decline of faith and practice in Europe and America since Vatican II implies something more basic than merely an ordinary falling away of Catholics that has been present in many eras.

The intellectual strength of the Church does not arise from Catholic universities or seminaries in any cohesive or organized fashion. On the other hand, there exist many pockets of intelligence, often individuals, sometimes groups, who have managed to get it right, both about the meaning of intelligence and the reasons why it is so difficult to be accepted in the public order. There have been a remarkable number of conversions, particularly in light of the disarray of the main-line Protestant Churches, but also from among the Evangelicals.

There are no moral, biblical, scientific, psychological, or historical questions regarding the faith and its intrinsic intelligibility that do not have sensible and adequate analyses and answers. The "conflict" of faith and reason is over. There is no conflict. What there is, I think, is a personal and cultural effort not to see that this compatibility not only exists but is the best available explanation of things. The sudden spate of "atheist" apologists strikes me as desperate attempts to avoid the obvious.

But the next decades, I think, will not be concerned so much with the intellectual side of the Western soul as with its own unwillingness to face the truth that all the alternatives it has systematically concocted do not work. The effort of the present pope to rediscover reason and natural law is first addressed to the soul of Europe, to remind it that it has not found an alternative to the heritage of Greek *logos* and Christian *caritas*. We gradually realize that our most important external problem, rapidly becoming an internal one, is Islam, its claim to truth and its remarkable closed-ness. But beyond that, as Islam itself seems to grasp, is the rest of the world.

The Christian faith, as Ernest Fortin once pointed out, has not really much surpassed the confines of the old Roman Empire and the colonies it sent out in the early stages of modernity. From now on, the intellectual strength of Catholicism, to be what it is, will find itself directed precisely to the other cultures, the initial approach to which will be through philosophy, through the fact that there is but one truth to which revelation itself is addressed precisely as a truth that completes truth. There is today a surprising dynamism within Catholicism that transcends its cultural weakness, itself based in one form or another on a denial of the real genius on which the faith is addressed to reason.

All cultures, including our own, need redemption for their sins. The real difficulty is not so much in knowing what the truth is, but in practicing it. The Christian faith does not think that one generation exists so that another generation down the line will be perfect. In that sense, no generation stands closer to God than another. All are judged by what they know and freely choose to do. It is interesting how often recent popes come back to this theme, that the one thing God cannot do in pursuing our redemption to everlasting life is to take away our freedom.

The drama of our times can often be stated to mean the specific rejection of the way to salvation through suffering and repentance that has been put into the world with the Incarnation of the Son of God. In *Jesus of Nazareth*, Benedict often came back to this simple but graphic point, that Jesus was true man and true God, the Son of Man, the Son of God. The reality of this presence is the single most important event in our race's presence on this earth. In one sense, we have done everything we can to prevent this truth from being recognized. On the other hand, and this is the intellectual strength of Catholicism, all arguments against the proper understanding of this truth themselves prove, in the end, to be inconsistent with themselves. This is more than a paradox. It is an event in history that remains there for us to understand its origins in the inner life of the Godhead.

Chapter 5

"The state now often realizes that one way to control the Church is through financing its charitable institutions to such a degree that they cannot operate without government funds."

Interview at Acton Institute (AI) with James V. Schall, S.J. (JVS)[*]

Question #1): (AI) What is the most common misconception that Christians make today about how effectively to help the poor?

Answer #1): (JVS) The most common mistake, and there are others, that Christians make is that poverty is primarily a problem of maldistribution of existing goods. The mere fact that some have more than others is itself, wrongly, taken to be a sign of injustice. Thus, the solution is simple: All we have to do is take over the excessive goods of some and give them to the others who have need of them. The primary institution assigned to carry out this justifying redistribution is the modern state. Probably no idea, except perhaps ecology, gives the state more unrestricted power than such ideas about poverty. In the end, it is claimed, everyone will be "equal." No one will have any reason to envy anyone else who, for whatever reason, has more than he does. The end of this mentality, if put into effect, would be quickly to make everyone poor, with little awareness that they could or should be anything else.

Q. #2): (AI) Scripture speaks of the poor and how we are to care for "the least of them." Do we keep this witness properly balanced today?

A. #2): (JVS) Poverty is not the only or most important topic mentioned in Scripture. Solomon did build a beautiful temple. It was rebuilt after it was first destroyed. Jesus Himself was in the Temple chatting with

[*] Interview published on-line, *Religion & Liberty*, V. 23, #3, Acton Institute, February 10, 2014.

the Learned of the Law. Jesus's concern with the poor assumed that there were those about who were not poor. Otherwise, they could not help the poor. I am always astonished at how often people who talk of poverty fail to talk of how wealth, whereby poverty can be lessened or eliminated, is produced and justly distributed in the first place.

In the parable of the talents, Christ seems annoyed at the man who buried his talent and did not increase it by investment like the others. Paul said that the man who would not work, should not eat. Were Paul to say that today, he would be accused of being insensitive. Paul at least showed that he was aware of freeloaders who really did little to earn their keep, yet who demanded to be taken care of by others. If everyone is absolutely poor, no one can help anyone, not that the poor sometimes cannot or do not help each other.

Poverty is mainly a comparative thing. The very rich think they are poor compared to the very, very rich. The poor think they are better off than the very poor. The question of poverty cannot be discussed as if the problem of how to produce wealth did not come up or as if we do not know something about how to produce wealth. Most poverty is caused by the refusal or inability to learn how to produce sufficient wealth so as not to be poor. Not a few modern ideologies, designed to help the poor, in fact imprison them in customs or institutions that cannot produce wealth. Some beliefs, such as the voluntarist position that there is no stable order, make it impossible to do what needs to be done to produce wealth by the work of our minds and hands.

Q. #3): (AI) Is there inherently anything "virtuous" about poverty?

A. #3): (JVS) Socrates, though he seems to have had enough to eat and at least a tunic and a home for his wife and boys, considered himself poor. But he thought of his poverty in terms of its freeing himself from the entanglement of wealth-getting. He held that his time was better spent in discussing the higher things. The religious vow of poverty is more in this Socratic tradition. It is not designed to make everyone poor. What it is designed to do is show that complete absorption in the things of this world is not really what will make us happy.

But poverty, especially voluntary poverty, is a tricky business. We cannot go around saying, "See how poor I am, look at me!" Poverty is poverty. We need not be rich. We can live a full human live with relatively few things. Aristotle rightly said, however, that most people need a sufficient amount of material goods to live a normal and virtuous life. The world was not given to us that we do nothing with it but sit around lamenting how poor we are. It really was given to us in a certain astonishing abundance. But we have to learn what this abundance is and how to develop it. That is why we are here.

Poverty is best reduced and eliminated when we are figuring out how to do and develop many things that we need and want, things of beauty and safety and health and everything else. The basic Christian teaching was not that we should make everyone poor, but that even the poor could ultimately save their souls. But in itself, the world was a challenge to make everyone rich through human action and intelligence.

Q. #4): (AI) Do you think an abundance of material goods, especially in the West, has also helped to promote a spiritual poverty?

A. #4): (JVS) It has been the experience of the classic Greeks, Hindus, and Chinese, I think, that an abundance of material goods enabled them to produce great and beautiful things. But it has also led to a system of control whereby rigidity set in. Slavery or its equivalent often had an economic basis, as Aristotle understood. If we had machines to do our work, he thought, we would not need slaves. This is pretty much what has happened.

But one of the things that an abundance of material goods makes us realize, as Aristotle also understood, was that riches were not happiness as such. At best, riches were aids, but they were not the end. Hence, it became possible to see that a life spent in pursuit of riches, with no further purpose, was an empty life. It was only when riches had a higher purpose that their real worth was seen. Moreover, as I mentioned, the Socratic tradition taught us to examine our lives. If we did so, we would discover that riches were at best helps and at worst temptations.

In themselves, riches were a good thing. There is nothing ignoble in thinking that everyone should live in abundance. It is interesting in recent years how much poverty has in fact been eliminated in the world. Many nations that were for centuries poor have learned something of how to produce wealth. Much of the talk about poverty today overlooks the fact of this rather amazing progress.

But the notion of spiritual poverty is a tricky one. As I recall, Mother Teresa used that phrase in the sense that many of the richest people in the world were "spiritually" poor. In one sense, only a rich man can really understand the emptiness of wealth if he thinks it is the final definition of his happiness. This was Aristotle's point in the first book of his *Ethics*. There is a reason why we might think wealth is the essence of happiness. After all, we can buy, we think, pleasures or honors with it. But when we have them, we soon discover that these things are themselves only means. So in that sense, riches themselves can lead to a sense of voluntary poverty, to the realization that our true end is not located in how much we own or have.

On the other hand, as Aristotle also said, once we understand the proper place of riches, if we have them, we can use them for good and noble purposes. This is what I think was implicit in Scripture but rarely mentioned, namely, that the rich were being taught what to do with their riches so that those who had were directed to the poor, not to keep them poor but to assist them in being not poor.

Q. #5): (AI) Many people are poor through no fault of their own, but this is not true of everyone. Do we have a problem with not blaming poverty on the forces that are sometimes the most responsible?

A. #5): (JVS) We do have a problem here. How often do people who talk of "helping the poor," in the logic of their complaint, demand that something be done about it? The next thing we find is that they are really demanding that governments do something. Yet, it is precisely governments that are often the most irresponsible agents, the ones that dry up the sources of wealth production. Governments are often the one agency most responsible for poverty in the name of getting rid of it.

Unions also are widely praised as giving "rights" to workers, whereas in fact they are partly responsible in their demands in shipping whole industries to other parts of the world. It becomes too costly to produce what others can and will produce more cheaply and in fact often better. This is a quagmire, I know. In one sense, it is in the interest for the alleviation of poverty that countries that were long stagnant suddenly learn how to work, to do the things that others do too expensively.

The high costs of labor in one country mean the possibilities of jobs in another part of the world. It is ironic that the rapid growth of economies in the world is due to the work ethic or intelligence of those in other parts of the world who had been cut off from modern means of production. One of the answers to this issue is to empower the state to prevent such jobs from going elsewhere. When this happens, the ethos of local labor becomes enforced and its high cost is not allowed to be challenged by competition.

I often wonder about the emphasis on "consumerism" that several popes have made. This consumerism is presumably a vice of demanding ever more goods for their own sake. Pope Francis talks of a "throw-away" society. But he also talks of the jobs that the young need. Rarely do popes talk of where such jobs come from. Basically they come from a sound economic theory and from minds. The ultimate riches are not land or resources. They are in the mind. That is the real source of wealth in the world.

We cannot have jobs unless we have people to consume what is produced. Men have to be able, hopefully by their own work, to purchase what they need and want. The obsolescence of things is not a bad thing in itself. The need of a market, of someone to consume, of producing something better, is absolutely necessary if we are going to talk of jobs. To say that we just need jobs without a word about where jobs come from is irresponsible. Moreover, to produce artificial jobs, or jobs that are in effect meaningless, for no purpose, is equally corrupting.

Q. #6): (AI) Catholic Charities receives a lot of funding from government programs. Is this type of funding ultimately of a positive or negative benefit?

A. #6): (JVS) One of the things Church people have had difficulty in understanding is that the culture itself can contain within it rules, customs, laws, or decrees that approve actions that are in fact contrary to good sense or Christian teaching. To become dependent on government programs is thus not a neutral thing. In the name of "greater good" one often finds himself justifying this aid. Pope Benedict in *Deus Caritas Est* put his finger on an important aspect of this problem. What government aid cannot do is to deal with the individual as such. Charity is not a bureaucratic virtue. People need more than aid. The reason Catholics are involved in such issues is primarily beyond politics.

This issue becomes especially difficult as we see the state more and more claim control of all aspects of the society, including religious organizations, which have anything to do with government monies or purposes. The popes have valiantly striven to show why faith has also a proper place in public. But as the public space becomes more alien to its practices and principles, it becomes clear that the government takes control of what it finances. It has used religious organizations because they are presumably better able to deal with certain issues of poverty or well-being than government bureaucracies.

But as many "rights" are now said to be necessary, to participate in their fostering is itself something that would undermine what the Church teaches. So the price is heavy. The state now often realizes that one way to control the Church is through financing its charitable institutions to such a degree that they cannot operate without government funds. Church bureaucrats themselves often seem willing to compromise principle to retain the funding. So yes, there are definitely positive and negative aspects here. The day seems fast coming in which the government, like other absolutist governments, simply takes control of all aspects of life—education, health, leisure, work, and culture, all of this in the name of helping the poor and the citizens.

Q. #7): (AI) What is the biggest hurdle in alleviating poverty today?

A. #7): (JVS) Probably, and paradoxically, the idea that we all should be poor in the name of Christianity, ecology, or limits of growth. I have asked the question recently, "Does Christianity want people to be poor?" I think that many religious people, using ecology and exploitation theory, do think this. And if we do want everyone to be poor, the best way to do this is to empower that authority whose normal ways will guarantee widespread poverty, namely the state, which in no way produces wealth itself. There is a certain attractiveness to this view. It is the view of Castro's Cuba. He has made a potentially prosperous country simply poor and declared them happy. He has successfully blamed all their ills on foreigners. Most Cubans who can get out do get out. But those who have to stay must say in public that they are happy and live a superior life to the rich elsewhere.

There is a tendency to want everyone to take a vow of poverty as a solution to our problems. Instead of asking how wealth is produced and distributed justly and effectively, we give up and claim that our purpose is to protect the planet for future generations. This protection means that we cannot use anything much. Best to leave it untouched for someone in 3456 AD. The trouble with this approach is that we have no idea what we can do with this earth. The amazing things that have happened with regard to energy and science in the past hundred years make us suspect that there are ways to make everyone rich that we have no suspicion of. We are afraid to know what we can know. This is why I say that the only basis of wealth is mind.

We need a more Aristotelian approach that recognizes that the establishment of a full and beautiful city is what we ought to be about. But at the same time, we are open to the transcendence that comes to us from revelation as it is addressed to our reason. We know that we have here no lasting city. We are at a stage, I sometimes suspect, where, in the name of poverty, we will cut off any possibility of everyone becoming not poor. The purpose of Christianity was that we save our souls no matter what sort of civil society we found ourselves in. But that did not take away a possible inner-worldly purpose that would really reach the human perfections of beauty, abundance, and well-being that are implicit in our creation and the relation of our minds to it.

Chapter 6

"Chesterton's 'spirituality' was very earthy, that is, incarnational. He liked beer and wine, bacon and eggs, and all things good. He thought that the only proper way to thank God for these good things was by not eating or drinking too much of them."

Interview by Sean Dailey (SD) with James V. Schall, S.J. (JVS)*

Question #1): (SD) How old were you when you first encountered Chesterton? What was the first book you read?

Answer #1): (JVS) Actually, I do not know the first book of Chesterton that I read or even when, but it was probably after I entered the Jesuits here at Los Gatos. The fine library of classics that we had in this house was just shipped, alas, to a house of studies in Nairobi, where I am sure they can use it. That library contained many Chesterton and Belloc books; this would have been 1950–52. When I went north to Spokane and philosophy studies at Mt. St. Michael's (Gonzaga University, 1952–55), I know that I was reading much Chesterton during the three years I was there. In fact, from that time, I cannot recall when I was not reading something of Chesterton. I certainly have not read everything the man wrote, which I consider a pity, a blessing, and perhaps impossibility.

Some good things you simply do not want to finish. Others you find that even if you read them once, the reading of them again is more illuminating than the first time you read them. I have always found this with Chesterton. I have written columns in *The Midwest Chesterton Review* or *Gilbert Magazine* either monthly or bi-monthly ever since. The man is inexhaustible. I think of Chesterton in the same way I think of Aquinas; both died with much left to say. But both knew that what they did say was, to

Interview in *Gilbert Magazine*, 17 (January/February 2014), 12–16.

use Aquinas's famous words, was but "straw" compared to the depths of God which awaited them.

Q. #2): (SD) How has Chesterton informed your life as a priest, a Jesuit, and a scholar?

A. #2): (JVS) The basic word that describes Chesterton is probably "sanity." I just had a letter from a former student who read a book the gist of which was that we would succeed in life if we "had confidence in ourselves." As I looked at that phrase, I recalled the passage in *Orthodoxy*, in the chapter on "The Maniac," I think, in which Chesterton remarked that the only person who has complete confidence in himself is the madman. After you read him for a while, Chesterton almost becomes second nature to you. I wrote a long essay in the journal *Telos* on the occasion of the 100th anniversary of the publication of *Orthodoxy* in 1908. I thought then, and I think now, that no greater book has been written since.

Orthodoxy simply puts all things together, including the final things. I cannot tell you how many times I have cited or reflected on the final words of *Orthodoxy*, that the only thing that Christ did not reveal to us was His "mirth." It was not because Christ did not see the delight in things, including human things, but because He did. Chesterton's point was simply that we could not bear the full delight for which we are created and destined until we reached eternal life. The real temptation is not that we have been given too little, but that we have been given so much. And the key word is "given," gift. Chesterton teaches us to see that the whole world is shot through with more than we could possibly expect.

I have never considered Chesterton to be a mere "scholar." Scholars are often trained to see the insignificant and specialized things. Chesterton saw everything. If philosophy is a knowledge of the whole, then Chesterton is a philosopher and a great one. Moreover, Chesterton was amusing. I have often laughed at and cited the quip of Chesterton to the lady who complained that his work could not be "serious" if it was also funny. Chesterton replied: "Madam, the opposite of serious is not funny. The opposite of funny is not funny." That is to say, no reason in the world can be found why truth and humor do not go together. If there is laughter on earth, how much greater will it be in heaven.

The proper reaction to truth is not solemnity but delight. Chesterton is the remedy to methodological scholars who, as so many do, fail to see how all things fit together. Chesterton was no "scholar." He was just an extraordinarily intelligent man who read about everything. He saw *the things that are*, affirmed them, rejected what was wrong, and laughed with his friends about the wonder of it all. He seems to have been admired and loved by most everyone, even those whose thought, as he wrote, was most odd or most silly.

Q. #3): (SD) You taught political philosophy at Georgetown until your retirement a year ago. What were some of the highlights of your career? What were some of the low points?

A. #3): (JVS) The highlight of any academic career is, I think, finally figuring out just what it is that you are doing or thinking. You begin to suspect that you have something to say that no one else can or will say. You get around to writing what you think, only to suspect you see more than you are capable of seeing. One picture of academia is that a young professor arrives at a university, fashions his field and style. He then teaches the same thing over and over down the years until his retirement. Yet, it is precisely in the opportunity to see the same things over and over again that one begins to see more than he ever realized was there as a young scholar. As C. S. Lewis said, it is only in the thirty-fifth reading that we finally catch a glimpse of all that was there.

It was my good fortune to have good students over the years, actually several thousands of them. Most of them never really heard of a tradition of reason and revelation that makes sense. They may know parts but not why it all fits together. This "fitting together" was in fact the theme of my book, *The Order of Things*. In fact, students do not think that things do or can fit together until they read their way through the books that make sense of things, which is what a university should be about.

So, I suppose the highlight of any academic experience is the day a professor notices that one of his students is paying attention, not so much to what he is saying, but to what both he and the student are reading together in Plato or Aristotle or Aquinas or Cicero. *A pari*, I suppose that the low point is the day a student, in evaluating the class, claims that he was bored and learned nothing much so that he did not try. He wanted to "learn" something other than what Thucydides or Augustine or Shakespeare had to tell him. And in truth he probably did learn something else.

Q. #4): (SD) Recently, a group of Georgetown alumni led by novelist William Blatty filed a canon law suit against the university, alleging that it has abandoned its Catholic identity. Would you care to comment on that?

A. #4): (JVS) Such procedures exist in Canon Law. People are certainly free to use them. The Church, in fact, encourages the laity to bring to the attention of bishops and Roman officials serious problems existing in their area. The Church is usually slow to respond, primarily because it must have the facts investigated and judged. Since such questions are brought up concerning almost every Catholic institution of higher learning, it would probably be good for everyone concerned to have some further clearing of the air. Given the wide variety of political and economic situations in which any Catholic institution must survive in this world, I would be surprised if anything more than a procedural response is given to this particular suit.

That we can have Catholic institutions at all is today more and more put in doubt by our secularized political culture, itself more and more a pseudo-religion brooking no opposition to its policies. But if the Church in a formal mode thought that Georgetown or any other institution was in no way Catholic, I am sure responsible folks would want to know about it.

Q. # 5): (SD) The next question should come as no surprise to you. What are your thoughts on Pope Francis? Of him being the first Jesuit Pope? Of the name he took, the founder of the first great mendicant Order?

A. #5): (JVS) Well, in a short time Pope Francis has certainly become a well-known figure to almost everyone. He certainly strives to greet everyone he can. I suppose by now that I have written some twenty or twenty-five columns or essays on one or another aspect of his words, deeds, and influence. Pope Francis seems to be in the news almost every other day with something.

Since it has taken some four hundred years to come around to a "first" Jesuit pope, it may take that long for another, so it need not be a present concern! The same can be said with the name "Francis." Some want to call him Francis I, but again, whether there will be a Francis II, we do not know. Whoever thought there would be sixteen Benedicts or twenty-three Johns, let along thirteen Leos and twelve Piuses? Indeed, some folks even seem to think that Francis is the last pope, the so-called "Petrus Romanus." But I am not going to worry about that. Given Pope Francis's style and views, Francis is the right name for him. The Church has been extraordinarily blessed in its popes in modern times, almost as if someone "up there" is looking out for it.

Q. #6): (SD) The preliminary stage of Chesterton's cause—the investigation at the diocesan level—began late last summer. What are your thoughts on this? Based on your knowledge of Chesterton and his writings, what do you think of him as an example of holiness? An example of lay spirituality?

A. #6): (JVS) Actually, I think that Chesterton should be considered under the category of a Doctor of the Church. If I read *Orthodoxy* at all accurately, Chesterton not only had a kind of dark night of the soul as a young man, but he really saw the truth of Catholic things before he was formally a Catholic. He tells us that it was not the Catholics who caused him to become Catholic, but the heretics who kept explaining what was wrong with the Church. In the end, he discovered what we discover every day, namely that opposition to the Church eventually exhausts itself of real intellectual reasons.

Much opinion begins to oppose the Church just to oppose it because it does not want to admit that the Church is right even if its opponents can give no more reasons for their opposition. It was the "heretics" who made Chesterton Catholic. In these dialogue and ecumenical days, we are loathe to affirm the truth of the faith. We only talk of what we have "in common," which usually means that we talk of everything but what the Church is to hold about itself. Chesterton spoke both about what was common and what was uniquely true.

Chesterton's spirituality was very earthy, that is, incarnational. He liked beer and wine, bacon and eggs, and all things good. He thought that the only proper way to thank God for these good things was by not eating or drinking too much of them. His was a world of appreciation for what was given to him. He was a faithful husband and loved babies and children even if he and his wife had none of their own. Eugenics appalled him, as did divorce. His book on the family, on man, woman, child, and education is prophetic (*What's Wrong with the World*).

But the really great thing about Chesterton is the clarity of his mind. I have found over the years that you can take almost any paragraph or chapter or essay of Chesterton and, when you unravel what he has implied in a few short sentences, you see the whole of reality in a different way. You see it as *it is*. You see, as he says memorably in his book on Aquinas, that "eggs is eggs." The word "*is*" is crucial for him, as it was for Aquinas along with the Book of Genesis and Moses for that matter.

The mind, Chesterton thought, was not made to doubt but to affirm, to state the truth it knew. We want to know the truth of things. And we can know it. In *The Everlasting Man*, Chesterton noted that the whole history of mankind reads like a story. And if there was a story, there had to be a story-teller. The idea of things coming from nothing is unintelligible, unless the nothing simply means that God has not yet created. Once He has created, what exists is there for us to know and work out our salvation.

Chesterton loved the common man, the man for whom revelation was also addressed. Chesterton suspected that his grandfather knew more philosophy than Nietzsche when he said that he (his grandfather) said that he would thank God for his life even if he ended in Hell. The Devil in Hell did not evidently thank God but instead goes around "seeking those whom he may devour." Chesterton really had more trust in the common sense of the common man than he did the learned sense of the intellectuals. In this, he was rather closer to St. Paul's worries about the aberrations of the philosophers. Likewise, Chesterton trusted those who owned their own property and thought we should have more of them. He did not think riches, as such, were bad, but he did think that the most dangerous moral environment was the one the rich lived in.

Chesterton's *Autobiography* begins with a spoof on modern biblical criticism. He tells us that he has no "proof" for his own existence. Even though he was apparently there at the time, he has no recollection of his birth but must depend on the testimony of others. His point is, of course, that depending on the testimony of others is not, *ipso facto*, irrational but makes good sense. Christianity depends on the testimony of the Apostles and on those to whom its truth has been handed down.

Chesterton's common sense thus shows itself everywhere. When speaking of evolution and the drawings in early caves, Chesterton said that it was not like some ape began the drawings and some evolved cave-man came along later to finish them. The whole project was human from the beginning. In other words, what Chesterton stands for is the reasonable human mind looking at the claims and theories that would, if carried out, make man inhuman. And while he laughs at such silliness, he sees the deadly logic for mankind that is ever present when the truths of reason and revelation are denied. Chesterton said that the purpose of the human mind is to affirm dogmas, that is, to state the truth of things.

At the end of *Heretics*, he wondered whether in the future, that is in our time, it would take faith even to say that grass is green. Without faith, man would become so disconnected with reality that he could see nothing in front of him but what his own mind had concocted. This indeed is what has happened. That is why I, at least, still read Chesterton with delight. I like the green grass and the blue sky. I too want to be among those who "have seen and yet believed."

Chapter 7

"I suspect the greatest love of one's life is the discovery of the origin of love in the Trinitarian inner life of the Godhead, the only possible place that the friendships we begin in this world could be completed and abide."

Interview by Sean Salai, S.J. (SS) with James V. Schall, S.J. (JVS) on "The Lost Art of Essay Writing."*

Question #1): (SS) Why did you write this book?

Answer #1): (JVS) Books that are collections of essays, I think, almost write themselves. That is, you will write one essay on some topic, than another on something else. But there is a certain mood to what you are saying. After four, five, ten, twenty, forty essays, you begin to wonder if they should not be collected into a single volume. For any book that you write, it is first and foremost your hope that someone, someday will read it. You have to be vain enough and humble enough to realize that surely someone will read it and realistic enough not to fall apart if no one does.

Q. #2): (SS) Who is your audience?

A. #2): (JVS) I once wrote a book called *Christianity and Politics*. About twenty years after it was published, I received a letter from a man in Brisbane, Australia. He told me that he came across the book in the back of his local parish church. He was a working man and he liked it. Somehow, the idea of that book making it to Australia made me realize what an "audience" was all about.

I recall that the great Father Joseph Fessio, while speaking of his experience in the publishing business, remarked to me that the remarkable thing about a book is precisely that you never really know who will read it or

---

* Interview by Sean Salai, S.J. on *The Classical Moment* with James V. Schall, S.J., in *America Magazine*, on-line, January 20, 2014.

when or even if. Books are not exactly immortal as physical objects—my fifty-year-old books are getting musty and brownish. But books have a way of remaining in place waiting for someone to read them. Christopher Morley once said that books are the most explosive things in the world. They just sit there waiting to go off. So, your audience is whoever chances to read what you write. The idea of being able to say or to identify just who exactly will read your book seems to encroach on a divine privilege.

Once, as a scholastic, while I was teaching at the University of San Francisco, I walked across campus one evening with Father Edmund Smyth. He had a doctorate in history from Toronto, as I recall. He told me that it was not unusual that a good scholar might spend his whole life writing a book or two that only four or five others in the world could properly understand. But it was imperative that we have the freedom and leisure to have such works. In the end, they may be the ones that save us.

But I am not averse to having books, like those of C. S. Lewis or Chesterton, that sell millions of copies well beyond their lifetimes. I suppose Augustine's *Confessions* is a classic example of such a book. Surely Augustine would be astonished at the audience that has, over the centuries, actually read the account of his life. Yet, even though the book is a colloquy with God, much of the world still reverberates with wonder at this book. I have always thought that Augustine definitely had me in mind when he wrote his *Confessions*.

Q. #3): (SS) What do you want people to take away from this new essay collection?

A. #3): (JVS) In a way, I do not want them to take anything with them. I want them to be amused, alerted, sometimes provoked, and always made aware of a look at things that they could never see but through my essay. Josef Pieper, that most insightful man, in commenting on Aquinas, once compared the essay form to the "article" form of St. Thomas. He pointed out that a good short essay and an article in the *Summa* were about the same length, three or four pages. The article set about to answer a question and give reasons for it, and to come to a conclusion. The essay, the "effort" in French, was looser. It could range widely over its subject matter. It did not have to be tightly argued. Yet, without the article, the essay is in danger of being fuzzy and frivolous, whereas, at its best, the essay contains genuine truths and deep feelings about human things, yes, even divine things.

Q. #4): (SS) In the book, you call the essay "one of the greatest inventions of the human mind," frequently quoting people like Samuel Johnson. Outside of newspaper op-eds, has essay writing become a lost art today?

A. #4): (JVS) As a matter of fact, essays are flourishing on the internet, to where so many magazines and reviews have migrated. There are remarkably good essays on The Catholic Thing, Crisis Magazine, University Bookman, Catholic World Report, and a huge variety of various blogs and websites. David Warren's "Essays in Idleness" is worth a hundred TV news broadcasts. As far as I can see, the art of essay writing is blooming. And I would add, like anything else, to have one really good essay, and one good collection of essays, we need to have hundreds that are not so good, but still pretty good and worth reading. So essay writing is by no means a lost art. It may be more dynamic today than at any time in history.

But I do think the essay is one of the great inventions of the human mind. It is not the only thing the human mind has invented, but it is one that, in a brief space, manages to say many things, sometimes serious, sometimes lightsome, and sometimes whimsical. The essay is always on some aspect of our lot that we might otherwise have missed.

Johnson, of course, was one of the great essay writers. I like the classical essays, which seem to have been invented or at least popularized by Montaigne, though Cicero, Seneca, and Horace are still great models and preserver of the form. I do a series of columns over the years in *The University Bookman* called "On Letters and Essays." I associate letters and collections of letters—like Flannery O'Connor's *The Habit of Being*—to belong together with essays. I am not sure if there is a collection of "Selected E-Mails," but that is the form in which the old letter written on paper seems to be going. The good thing about a printed copy of a book and a journal is that you can hold them in your hands. Somehow, that seems more permanent, even though, if I want to look up Dorothy Sayers's "Lost Tools of Learning," I do so on some search engine even though I have several printed copies of it somewhere in my files.

Q. #5): (SS) Why us the essay still relevant?

A. #5): (JVS) Why is anything still relevant? I am afraid that I consider the criterion of "relevancy" to be one of the great causes of university mediocrity. It is a version of "keeping up with the Joneses." The essay is a form, not the only one, to be sure, in which you can tell the truth. We need this "telling" perhaps more than anything in our culture. Moreover, as Chesterton said, there is no reason why an essay cannot be funny and tell the truth at the same time. He said in a memorable phrase, when he was accused of not being serious because he was amusing, that the opposite of funny was "not funny." Many of the greatest truths we know are also funny and delightful. The essay should not be defended on the grounds that it is "relevant" but on the grounds that is one very concise way to tell the truth.

Q. #6): (SS) In your opinion, who are the best essayists in current writing?

A. #6): (JVS) The best essayist in the English language, as I have argued in my recent book, *Remembering Belloc*, is Belloc. And the good thing about the essay is that it does not make any difference when the essay was written. There is absolutely no reason why "current writing" should be a criterion for our attention to essays. As I mentioned above, I think that we are living in a time of great flourishing of essays. I like David Warren, Joseph Epstein, Thomas Howard, Joseph Pearce, and George Will.

But when I sit down to read an essay, I usually reach for Belloc, C. S. Lewis, or Johnson. I refuse to be imprisoned by the now. I used to have a theme—"To be up-to-date is to be out of date.." If I write an essay, which I seem to have been doing most of my life, I do not compare it with "current writing." I go back and read an essay of Belloc and shake my head and say to myself, "This is just great!" I do the same when I reread Hazlitt's "On Going a Journey." "How could anything be better?" I ask myself.

I should also say a word about Plato. If someone asks me "Is Plato relevant?," I almost despair. Sometimes I am not sure anything else but Plato is worth reading. The subtitle of my book *Idylls & Rambles*—a title that obviously comes from Samuel Johnson's essay collections in *The Idler* and *The Rambler*—is "Shorter Christian Essays." Thus, I tend to distinguish between long and short essays. My love is the short essay. Some of my best essays though are longer ones, especially on Plato. In many ways my best academic essay is entitled "On the Death of Plato: Some Philosophical Thoughts on the Thracian Maidens," which is found in my collection, *The Mind That Is Catholic*.

I might add that I have been writing a series of essays called "Schall on Chesterton" for many decades now. Some of these are collected in CUA Press's book *Schall on Chesterton*. I would fail if I tried to explain the wonder of Chesterton's essays. I have a number of books that are more academic and not just collections of essays—*At the Limits of Political Philosophy; Reasonable Pleasures; The Order of Things; Reason, Revelation, and the Foundations of Political Philosophy; The Modern Age*; and *The Regensburg Lecture*. But I do love the essay, and all books begin with some small sketch that is really an essay.

Q. #7): (SS) You often mix pop-culture references into your essays, citing Charlie Brown and Snoopy as philosophers alongside Aristotle and Augustine. Why?

A. #7): (JVS) The short answer is that Charles Schulz is, in fact, a very good philosopher writing in a format that may be off-putting to the purist who cannot imagine true philosophical insight to appear in a cartoon. Actually, I never particularly liked Snoopy. I found the real core of Schulz in Charlie himself, particularly in Lucy, but also in Linus, Schroeder, and the others. I see nothing to prevent my citing any insight I might come across if it makes what I am saying clear or if it says the truth in a way that a few would otherwise miss.

Again, that is the genius of the essay form. You can include anything in it if it makes the truth in its own way. Msgr. Robert Sokolowski, who is probably the best philosopher among us, has a wonderful book entitled *Pictures, Quotations, and Distinctions*. He points out that our ability to cite someone else in the context of our own thinking or writing enables us to call on the rest of the world as we think our way through our own understanding of it. When you write, you write among both friends and antagonists. Of the latter, you want, as Aquinas would advise, to find the truth in what they are trying to say. Of the former, you are grateful that someone else has seen a truth before you did, or explained to you why it was so. So to "mix" these references is simply to be honest. Someone else really did guide you to some truth or insight that you might have otherwise never noticed.

Q. #8): (SS) You retired after 35 years as a popular Georgetown professor teaching classical political philosophy. If you could pick only one lesson that students took from your writing and teaching, what would it be?

A. #8): (JVS) The overwhelming thing, I suppose, is a lesson from Aristotle. That we cannot have many good friends in this life, that true friendship is for a few in a complete lifetime. Yet, and this is the Christian element, we still have met so many fine and lovely students that we only began to know. They each had to go on to their own lives. Yet, reality somehow cannot be at rest if it does not ultimately include this completion of what was also begun in this life. This is why I have written so much on immortality and resurrection. There is already much of this wondering in my first book, *Redeeming the Time*.

Still, with regard to students, I think that my book, *Another Sort of Learning*, best takes us to the lessons that students teach us. The function of a professor is primarily to teach the truth, not "his" own private truth. Students are just out there. When you walk into class the first day of a se-mester, they do not know you nor you them. They are not there so you can entertain them, though you hope that they laugh at your jokes, even if they are not particularly funny. You do not "own" the truth. You are there as someone who has read and hopefully pondered things that they never thought of, the things *that are*. You are there to enable them, as Yves Simon explained, to arrive at the truth faster than if they floundered about by themselves.

So you tell them about those books and writers who have helped you. *Another Sort of Learning* is full of books to read, books that probably no one ever told them about, books, as I say, "to keep sane by." But you read with them. They have heard of Aristotle, perhaps, but have no clue about him. So you just begin to read him. "Stick with me," you tell them, "you will see." Most often they do.

But you cannot "make" them see. It is something that must come from within them as it has to come from within you, but about something that is not you, about *what is*. So you look for what I call "the light in the eye." You look for the day that the young man in the back of the room suddenly seems to perk up. He seems to see that Aristotle or Plato or Aquinas has something to say.

You tell them that one of the things you want them to learn from your course is that the most exciting things they will ever encounter came from hundreds and thousands of years ago. They will find nothing quite like it and they know it. When they see this, your job as a professor is basically over. That is always why I tried to end my classes with Plato. As I say, there is no such thing as a university in which the reading of Plato is not con-stantly going on.

Q. #9): (SS) Outside of knowledge for its own sake, what is the greatest love of your life?

A. #9): (JVS) Goodness! "Knowledge for its own sake" is again Aristotle. Strictly speaking, we can only love what is loveable. Ideas we know. We want to know if they are true or not. But we can only love a person. And the love of persons includes, as Aristotle said, reciprocity. Once we realize this fact, we can begin to wonder why we are told that the first commandment is to love the Lord, our God.

This gets us to Aristotle's problem of whether God is lonely. We then read in Aquinas that there is otherness in God. A chapter in *Redeeming the Time* was called "God Is Not Alone." It was the chapter on the Trinity. I once heard the Australian writer and publisher, Frank Sheed, a famous speaker at Hyde Park Corner in London, say that the one topic that always caused silence and attention in these most critical listeners was that of the Trinity. I suspect the greatest love of one's life is the discovery of the origin of love in the Trinitarian inner life of the Godhead, the only possible place that the friendships we begin in this world could be completed and abide.

Q. #10): (SS) Any last thoughts?

A. #10): (JVS) We live in a time in which the very essence of our republic and our reason are being overturned in the public order. They are replaced by the voluntarism of which Pope Benedict spoke so clearly. All turmoil in the public order begins in the hearts and minds of the dons, clerical and academic. My last thoughts are those of Chesterton concluding *Heretics* in 1905. In the end, he said, the only ones left to uphold reason in the modern world will be the believers. We are seeing this happen before our very eyes, but few notice because few want to know.

Chapter 8

"What do we make, for instance, of the recent spate of books by atheists that attempt to use logic and reason to assert that there is, in the end, no source or meaning to logic or reason? Isn't that like a neo-Luddite using the internet to denounce technology?"

Interview by Carl Olson (CO) with James V. Schall, S.J. (JVS) on *The Order of Things* (San Francisco: Ignatius Press, 2007).*

Question #1): (CO) First, I'd like to wish you "Happy Birthday"! You turn eighty on January 20th. Any thoughts on that milestone?

Answer #1): (JVS) Carl, I am pleased you noticed the "milestone," as you called it. In *Crisis*, I did columns entitled "Schall at Seventy," "Schall at Seventy-Five," and one on "Schall at Eighty." In each one of them, I think, I cited the passage from one of the Psalms that reads "Man is given seventy years, and eighty if he is strong." Actually, aside from a few unpleasant incidents, I have been in good health most of my life.

I am older than most of my students' grandparents. Elizabeth II is two years older than I. Pope Benedict is six months older. His autobiography in fact is called *Milestones* (Ignatius 1998). The Pope discusses the relation of eternal life to this life in *Spe Salvi*. He says that nothing is wrong with wanting to live a long life. But we do not want to live to be one fifty or two hundred. The normal human span has its own purpose. Death is given as a punishment, but also as a blessing. We can clearly see the blessing part when we consider scientific efforts to abolish it in this world. They end up making us longer-lived and decrepit.

In the *Los Angeles Times* while I was at my niece's over Christmas, I read an article about the prima ballerina of the Cuban Ballet Company, a

---

* Interview by Carl Olson, with James V. Schall, S.J., in *Ignatius Insight*, January 2008.

lady also in her eighties. She said something about wanting to live to be two hundred. As she was a friend of Castro, she probably was a Marxist, which would mean that inner-worldly immortality would be the only sort available to her. The Pope pretty well spelled out the difficulties with such a view and with the scientific thinking behind it. It is largely an effort to escape the reality of eternal life by proposing a this-worldly life that goes on and on. What we really are made for and desire is "eternal life," as the Pope rightly called it.

We Americans live in almost the only country in the world where old age cannot as such be used as a means to retire us. This is, legally at least, the reason why Schall is still able to teach. Unlike those cultures where the elderly are welcome within the family, we do tend to put the elderly (and the young) in separate cantonments. "Retirement" is thus a rather interesting word. The activities of old age are a favorite topic of the classical authors.

We do begin to see, looking at Europe and in some sense ourselves, what happens to those cultures that cease to produce their own children. They age rapidly. They import other people's children to replace their own, which is usually called an "immigration crisis." The Europeans, when they dare to think about it, wonder who will defend them or take care of them, at what cost. They are quickly finding out. They live in suppressed fear of the future which they have given up and not replaced it with eternal life. What was it the Pope said at the *"Te Deum"* Vespers on the last day of 2007? "To say it in a word, in Rome one also notes that lack of hope and trust in life that constitutes the 'obscure' evil of modern Western society" (*Osservatore*, 2 January 2008).

With a class, I read the *Republic* of Plato every semester. Thus, I frequently think about the conversation in book 1 between Socrates and Cephalus in the old man's home in the Piraeus. He protests to Socrates that he is too old to come up to the city to listen to him. He complains that Socrates does not come down to see him. But Socrates tells him that he enjoys speaking with old men. Why? Because they have been down a road which we all must follow. I urge students to talk to their grandparents; it is all in Plato, who died at 81.

So we would like to know how it is down the years. Unexpectedly, Cephalus tells Socrates that he has not found it so bad. He acknowledges that most old men complain about loss of strength and pleasures. When Socrates suggests that the reason why Cephalus finds old age so tolerable is that he is rich. Cephalus admits that it is true that his wealth is of some assistance. For as we get older we begin to worry about whether we were really just in our lives. If not, we can repay our debts and perhaps pay to offer sacrifices.

Cicero takes up this same theme in his famous essay "On Old Age," an essay that shows us that great minds read what went before them. No essay looks at the reasons for a natural death better than Cicero. He also puts it in its context of a service to others. Wisdom is to be passed on but it cannot be passed on unless it is attained in the living of our lives.

Q. #2): (CO) This year, if I am not mistaken, marks another milestone of sorts for you: the fortieth anniversary of the publication of your first book. In 1968, after having co-authored a couple of books, the first book under your name alone was published: *Redeeming the Time* (Sheed & Ward). I own and have read that book, and it bears some interesting similarities to your most recent book, *The Order of Things*, especially in how it contemplates the Trinity, man in the world, and the nature of the cosmos. What similarities and differences do you see? Has your thinking about those Big Topics changed over the decades between?

A. #2): (JVS) I am pleased that someone has read both of these books. You are right; both are about "the Big Topics," what are often called the "highest things" by those who do not like to name God. I would include also in this list the Redemption and friendship as central themes. Ever since I began more carefully to think of political philosophy as such, largely since I arrived here at Georgetown, I have added the central theme of how reason addresses revelation and how revelation addresses reason. I have returned again and again to this fundamental topic. As *Spe Salvi* also points out, the whole "order" of modernity at its deepest roots is either an opening to revelation or, more often, a substitute for it.

Clearly, what fascinates me is the question of "how do things fit together?" I can still recall the thrill that I received when I read Stanley Jaki's book, *The Road of Science and the Ways to God*, when he pointed out that modern science could not have happened without a theology that allowed for real secondary causes that were not purely a product of the human mind. They had to be investigated by this same human mind to find out what they were. The mind "found" mind already there. Actually this issue of secondary causes is what is behind much of the problems with Islam and its voluntarism. The reason this point is important, something I believe recognized by Whitehead, is that we do not have to set science against theology and revelation. They are aspects of the same ordered understanding of things.

I was thinking the other day that I should have included in *The Order of Things* a chapter on the "Order of Games." Now I have written several essays and two short books (*Play On: From Games to Celebrations* and *Far Too Easily Pleased: A Theology of Play, Contemplation and Festivity*) in which I have meditated on Aristotle's notion that games are "for their own sakes." I cannot tell you how often students have remarked to me, after reading the essay "On the Seriousness of Sports" in *Another Sort of Learning*, how relieved they were to discover that their inner fascination to watch good games was not just frivolous or a "waste of time." Quite the opposite, of course, it was something welling up from their very being seeking finally to confront *what is*, what finally is "for its own sake," what finally is simply fascinating because it is the good. We learn this latter from watching good games unfold before us.

Actually, it is the Trinity that has most fascinated me. All else flows from that source. What a remarkable relief it is to realize that God does not create the world because He "needs" it, as if He were somehow deficient. I think that is already implicit in *Redeeming the Time*. The other side of this question is the fact that Redemption, the coming of the Word into the world, is the central doctrine that corresponds to Aristotle's treatise on friendship which wonders whether God is lonely and whether friendship itself requires resurrection. In *Spe Salvi*, the Pope cited two members of the Frankfurter school who practically said that to solve humanity's ultimate problems, we need the resurrection of the flesh. For any friendship, we need flesh and its resurrection.

Has my thinking on such issues changed? To say, "No, Schall's ideas do not change, I know will sound either arrogant or rigid. "Rigid" is that modern word for any belief that there may just be truths that not only do not change, but that we do not want to change because we catch a glimmer of the truth. The universe we live in has both change and permanence within it. One of the functions of the intellect is to decide which is which.

Change for its own sake implies a denial of any purpose, no "change to what?" The very fact that all things, especially ourselves, are created to return to God after their own manner is what is behind the real dynamism in the universe. If we finally managed to get to heaven only to find out nothing was there but "Change," a view already implicit in Heraclitus, I suspect we would despair. If we didn't, we should, for it is not heaven where we find ourselves where all things are changing without end.

Speaking of milestones, this year is also the hundredth anniversary of the publication of Chesterton's *Orthodoxy*. This is really the greatest book published in the last hundred years. Chesterton is always a delight to me, a delight of the mind. If someone reads *Orthodoxy* over and over again, which is certainly a pleasant thing to do, his mind will, I think, be in order; either that or he will have to rage and deny that either revelation or reason exists. He will hate *Orthodoxy* because it spells out the truths that are really behind the *things that are*.

Q. #3): (CO) A reader once asked me, "Does Schall ever sleep? The man must do noting but read and write!" (It was, of course, meant as a compliment). So, do you sleep? More seriously, what does, say, your average week look like, with teaching, reading, writing, praying, etc.? Do you set out to write a certain amount each day or week? Or does it just happen?

A. #3): (JVS) Rest assured, Carl, that Schall gets enough sleep. I pretty much cease to function if I do not. Besides, I am fond of sleeping, itself a gift of the gods. But this question about Schall's "busy-ness" must be viewed from the other side, which is, of course, my brother's side. My good brother Jerry is fond of asking the question, in front of friends, in his elder brother's presence: "Tell them how many hours a week do you college professors work?" I know there is no defense. I have read Plato on the view of the ordinary man on the life of the professor. "The answer," he tells them, "is six hours a week." He then adds, "Ask him what he does with the other 178 hours a week." It is a family joke, but it is also, in a way, your question, Carl. What does Schall do with the other hours of the week?

The answer is not simply "prepare class," though preparing class is one of the greatest incentives a mind can have. We professors are in great debt to the fact that those young students out there are willing just to be there and listen to us. But the answer to what one does the rest of the time is really straightforward: "I think about things." The only justification of a student attending a university or in a university existing at all is the chance of listening to the professor think about things, think about the truth of things, about *what is*.

When I have said these things, I always insist on citing the following line from Yves Simon, one of my heroes, a clearer mind hardly exists. Simon wrote: "No spontaneous operation of intellectual relations protects the young philosopher against the risk of delivering his soul to error by choosing his teachers infelicitously" (*A General Theory of Authority*, p. 100). The Christian theory of the fall hints that professors are more likely to err than any other group in our society, such is the nature of pride. Finding teachers who tell them the truth is in fact the main task of young students. In any university there are numerous pied pipers who lead us down paths no mind should follow. And they are charming. I have tried to suggest books that gently lead back to reality.

There is no way to convince anyone that teaching a "full academic" load of six hours a week is anywhere near a full time occupation. But a university is a certain kind of institution. Its "work," if you will, is not labor. It is what Pieper called leisure. I think that, if it does what it should, a university provides almost the only leisure, in the Aristotelian sense, left in our society. Academic departments try to quantify what professors do. But this is almost impossible to do. At their best, universities tell their professors, "Go ahead and see what you come up with." They are "free" places, as Pope Benedict intimated in his Regensburg Address. The old Jesuit Order had some of this sense of reducing prayer and community time to an absolute minimum in order that the life of the mind, itself both an individual and social good, could happen freely in real human beings. It cannot, for the most part, be programmed. It is easily abused, often corrupted.

A Catholic university, in its essence, is a place where thinking about *all that is*, including reason and revelation and all else, can be freely pursued. How many "Catholic" universities there are, I would not hazard a guess. But what is peculiar to such an institution is that the truths of the faith—Trinity, Creation, Redemption, the Virtues, yes, "the four last things," as *Spe Salvi* shows—are the things that are most exciting to think about in light of all the alternative proposals. I have always loved Aristotle's remark which I just reread today with a class: "For all the facts harmonize with a true account, whereas the truth soon clashes with a false one" (1098b11–121).

One has to have time to read, to write. Things jell. We can be too busy. But he also needs the incentive to do so, what Rebecca West once called "the strange necessity." I have always been struck in myself and in others by the fact that when you come across something that is strikingly true or strikingly funny, or both at the same time, the almost physical urge to tell someone else about it arises in our souls. Ultimately, I think, along with Plato, that this response to the truth we discover is why the world was created in the first place.

There is a "gladness" about teaching, I think. I have written a lot about the topic of students and teachers. But that gladness is best, I think, when a students tells you, on his own: "You know, Father, I never thought of that before, but it is true. I see it." He is not complimenting you on "your" truth. He has suddenly seen in his own soul the same truth that you saw, usually with the help of some obscure friend or writer, even the not so obscure ones like Aquinas and Augustine, who are still the best.

But I am not someone who writes a certain number of lines a day. I have often read of writers who have such a discipline. They write their four pages and take off for a beer or to mow the lawn. I find the "discipline," if that is what it is, which I doubt, in the idea itself, which is closer to pleasure and delight than anything else. I recall Gilson saying somewhere that you never know what you will write before you start to write. Your very writing is the working out of what you have to say. The very writing is the creating, the thinking through the issue that appears in your soul as a seed. Sometimes you even feel that it is not you who is writing. Writing is a habit that started long ago. "The strange necessity" to write something, likewise, never knows whether there is anyone out there to read it. But that is the mystical contract that a writer has with the world, living and dead and yet to be born.

I doubt if Carl Olson was born when *Redeeming the Time* was first written, speaking of milestones. As it fascinates me also, I never tire of pointing out to students, on reading them with me, the fact that Plato and Aristotle lived some twenty-five-hundred years ago. And yet, they are better than any other thing they will read. And I then ask, "Why is that?" Basically, it is because we live in the same world and our souls long for the same truth.

Q. #4): (CO) One thing that you seek to do—and you do it very well— is to introduce readers to the minds and thoughts of writers and thinkers they might not otherwise meet. In the first few pages of *Redeeming the Time*, for example, you mention or cite J. F. Powers, Pourrat, G. L. Prestige, Shelly, Dostoyevsky, Tolstoy, and E. M. Forester. Likewise, in the opening pages of *The Order of Things* you discuss Plato, C. S. Lewis, Belloc, Aquinas, Josef Pieper, Samuel Johnson, James Boswell, and (of course) Aristotle. Do you find that this approach to teaching and writing puts you at odds with the prevailing trends in education? How do students and readers react to it?

A. #4): (JVS) Yes, what I seek to do is to take readers to books and essays. Usually, I entitle my book lists something like "Twenty-Five Books that No One Will Ever Tell You About." Even though I am a reader of the so-called Great Books, the Platos, Aristotles, Aquinases, Machiavellis, Hegels, and Nietzsches, I am not really in the business of pursuing studies in texts or issues of scholarly *Wissenschaft*, however valuable that may otherwise be. I am interested in the whole. Philosophy is the knowledge of the whole, insofar as we can have it. And if we cannot have it all in this life, which we cannot, it is about knowing what we can. Socrates' "knowing that I know nothing" is nothing other than the negative theology principle that however much we can know about God, what we do not know is infinitely greater. But as the Pope said in the Regensburg Lecture, we really do know something even if we do not know everything. And that slim bond is what keeps all things together.

Often I tell the story of being a young man in the Army where, after a semester at college, with some leisure time, I went into the Post Library (at Fort Belvoir, Virginia, in fact). Looking over the stacks, I suddenly and vividly realized that *I did not know what to read!* Nor did I really know where to go to find out. But the impact of that realization was only brought home to me in later years after I had read some things. Now, this latter opportunity to reflect was only possible to me, in my particular circumstances, because I entered the Order at a time when we were taken off the streets ("out of the world," as it was quaintly put) for long years, really seventeen. We really did nothing much but read and reflect. Many a modern cleric thinks that sort of thing was absurd because it is the culture that is to educate us, that social justice is safe without philosophy. But I now have read Plato and Augustine, and I know better.

Moreover, I have been influenced by Aquinas, Chesterton, Lewis, and others in the view that the truth can be stated clearly and succinctly. It can also be stated charmingly. And, with Chesterton, there is no reason why what is true cannot also be funny. I have been much influenced by the notion that there is a joy behind things, something I found certainly in Chesterton and Belloc above all, but also in Flannery O'Connor, Charles Schulz, and all the humorists. P. G. Wodehouse writes many truths. Humor is, as I once wrote, close to sadness; but the converse is also true. I know that to be a Christian means to hold that in the end there is gladness, but only if we choose it. Not surprisingly that is often what we find out in our daily lives dealing with those we love and know.

You will recall the *Ignatius Insight* essay that you kindly did, "31 Questions for Schall" (10 October 2007). That essay was occasioned by my participating in a program at the University of North Dakota in which the student seminar read a number of my books—*A Student's Guide to Liberal Learning, Another Sort of Learning, On the Unseriousness of Human Affairs*, and *The Sum Total of Human Happiness*. When the seminar was over, the two professors who conducted it required a paper of the students reflecting on what they had read. Almost all of these students said the same thing that you did, namely, that Schall directs one to books that lead to other books that lead to truth. That is pretty close to what I have always thought that I was doing. The very title, *Another Sort of Learning*, with its long sub-title, was designed to tell students that they were not to despair if they did not learn anything really important or if they only were given ideology. Anyone can read. My friend Anne Burleigh says that this is the first freedom, the ability to read. And with that little blessing, anyone can read a few books to get him started. But some of these books are the best he will ever read, I think.

My book lists usually contain short, concise books. The first thing a young man or woman needs to do is wake up. I can read something that is important, true. Once this initial fire is kindled in our soul, we are all right. Plato has much to say about this, the "turnings around," the "what did you say, Socrates?," but also his warning that we often start too young. We are not ready to see or understand so we turn away. This in part is why I love to cite C. S. Lewis's remark that "if you have only read a great book once, you have not read it at all." I often describe my mission to students by saying, "It is the function of Schall to get you through the book the first time." The first time is often confusing and bewildering if someone is not there to urge the student on. That is, as I see it, why I am in a classroom and in fact enjoy being there. Over the years, I have had thousands of students in class. Samuel Johnson, another hero of mine, once remarked on what a delight this is to have them about. He was right.

Q. #5): (CO) Why a book on "order"? Isn't that considered a rather quaint, even restrictive, notion? Why not a book on "liberation" or "the politics of gender" or "self-expression"?

A. #5): (JVS) I did write a book once called *Liberation Theology*! Well, you cannot write a book on gender until you first decide what men and women are. Get this wrong and you will probably get everything else wrong. Indeed, you even first have to decide what grammar is. I have always thought one of my better books was *Human Dignity and Human Numbers*. That was written in the days when the literati thought that there would be too many of us. In the meantime, Paul VI wrote a prophetic encyclical in which he suggested that if you stop having babies, soon there will be too few of you. One of my most prophetic short essays was published in the old *Month* in London, in September 1969, entitled "The Papacy and Humor." I suspected even then that the papacy would have the last laugh, and it did.

It has always struck me as rather odd to be "expressing" oneself before one has anything to express or any check of reality on whether what one expresses had any object or truth. I am frankly put off by people who go about "expressing" themselves when their only claim for the worth-whileness of what they express is that they express it. All you can say to such a thesis is, "Well, fine, now what?" If my "expression" is true and so is yours, even if they are the opposites, then all that is left is universal incoherence.

But "order" is a different matter. If we take a look at the index of Aristotle's *Basic Works*, we see that everything is ordered. We know where things belong. I never forget the thrill I had when I first realized, and this was not too long ago, that there were really two worlds. The first was the natural world of things that could not be otherwise. This is the world that supports our existence, and includes the whole cosmos. The second is the world that could not exist without us, the world. This is the world full of our own choices, each of which could be otherwise. This is the world of "praise and blame," as Aristotle called it. The first, cosmic world is for the second, moral world. The ultimate purpose of the universe lies in this second world.

"Why a book on order?" you ask. We do not so much live in a world that betrays no order as in a world that maintains that even if there is an order we cannot know it. It is an epistemological problem. The various forms of relativism are the product of this view. But it has a moral origin, I think. Modern relativism is really an effort to protect us from having to face the truth that there has been a revelation which is addressed to a world that has reason. If this is the case, the only way to protect ourselves to be "free," in the sense of doing whatever we want, is to deny the power of reason to know anything.

I am a fan of Chesterton's notion that the real problem of the world in accepting a coherent order of things is that the truth is too good to be true. It is not so much that mankind does not want to know the truth, but it does not want to know it if it comes from a certain place which they have convinced themselves cannot know the truth. This means that they go off in their own order of disorder, as Aquinas put it. It is very strange, really.

The problem is not just that there is an order, but that we are intended to understand and acknowledge it as an order that ultimately does not come from ourselves. *The Order of Things* simply says that, even though we may want to deny that order exists in our lives and in our soul, the fact is that it is there. The reason we deny it is because we want only to live under our own order. As opposed to the order of joy of which Chesterton spoke, it is an order of sadness. The stakes are very high.

Q. #6): (CO) In the opening chapter, "The Orderly and the Divine," you point out something that often amuses and frustrates me at one and the same time. There remains, of course, those who find no order or reason in reality. They even, somewhat illogically perhaps, spend a good deal of time explaining why it is "reasonable" that there is no order or reason in things. What do we make, for instance, of the recent spate of books by atheists who attempt to use logic and reason to assert that there is, in the end, no source or meaning to logic or reason? Isn't that like a neo-Luddite using the internet to denounce technology?

A. #6): (JVS) The current "atheist" books have received am amazingly large number of highly critical reviews suggesting that the gentlemen atheists are rather superficial in their tastes and deficient in their logic. It is no longer possible to shock the world when some scientist announces in the *New York Times* or *Nature* that he is an atheist. Most people yawn and wonder what else is new. If you want to cause a stir suggest that there is something to "intrinsic design."

The atheist onslaught, if it is that, arises, I suspect, out of desperation. The notion that the whole universe has a very precise order as does everything in it, which the old determinists could accept, is not so much the problem with the current crop of atheists. They know that there is indeed an argument for intrinsic design. And this argument does not arise from religion. No, religion has long capitulated to the notion of "evolution." It is the scientists who have the problems with the notion that there is no order in a universe which seems not only to betray order at every step, but betray an order that seems designed to bring forth the rational creature someplace within this same universe.

In the "Regensburg Lecture," Benedict had a very penetrating remark. He was stating that the Church has no problem with science or its modern discovery if they have a proper human use. In fact, he said, the modern world was the result of a combination of "Plato and mathematics." Then he added that the world is not simply matter and therefore subject to the jurisdiction of mathematics, which presupposes matter. By restricting itself only to what could be analyzed by mathematics, science neglected to know those myriad of things that were not material, which the older religions and philosophies understood.

Benedict then remarked that it was rather curious that mathematics actually worked in the world. If we do not measure or calculate properly, the things we make fall down. Does it not seem odd that a correspondence exists between mathematics, from the tradition of Plato, that in fact applies to the real world? The world of ideas and the world of physical being seem to belong together. "Why?" the Pope wonders. He addresses himself to the scientists: "Does it not seem that they have a common origin that can be from either the world or our own minds?" Benedict leaves it at that. I suspect the current atheist books know very well what is at stake. They are no longer facing a philosophic and Christian mind (which is also itself philosophical) that does not know their game. The agenda of this Pope includes the minds of scientists on their own grounds.

Q. #7): (CO) There are chapters on "The Order within the Godhead," "The Order of the Cosmos," "The Order of the Soul," and "The Order of the Mind" (among others). But "The Order of Hell?" Please explain a bit.

A. #7): (JVS) Ah, you have caught Schall in his favorite Platonic topic, namely Hell. It is a place Schall would prefer not to visit, but is glad it is there, wherever there may be. Christ asked "How could Beelzebub's kingdom stand if it was not united?" The "order" of Hell is found in revelation. It is also found in philosophy. The great last book of Plato's *Republic* is precisely about the punishment due to those who persist in their evils. Christianity did not "invent" Hell. It was already in the Old Testament and in the Greeks.

Over the years, I have included a chapter on Hell in my books—*The Politics of Heaven and Hell, At the Limits of Political Philosophy*—as well as doing several essays on this happy topic. I even gave a talk called "The Hell It Is" at a pub in Stamford, Connecticut. And there is an essay on Chesterton in the *New Blackfriars* called "Haloes in Hell."

Now, I happen to think the doctrine of Hell, far from being that awful topic that all liberal thinkers think must be treated as an aberration, is the charter of our freedom. Without the doctrine of Hell, our lives would be utterly vapid and insignificant. Indeed, I have held, and the Pope touches on this same point in *Spe Salvi*, that modern political philosophy is nothing less, at times, than a constant recreation of Hells in this world as a result of its own dynamic. The gulags and the concentration camps, even the abortion clinics, are but this-worldly versions of Hell. They flow directly out of modern thought seeking to give us a perfect world by our own powers.

Basically, the doctrine of Hell means that each of our lives at every minute of our existence is infinitely important. Each of us can, if we choose, do an act against ourselves or others that can send us to Hell. This means, looked at from this angle, that our lives really are meaningful. The very drama of human existence is made poignant because of this divine insistence on its importance.

The "order" of Hell, I think, reflects the order of our actions. Those who reject the existence of Hell are logically left with an unjust world, the very purpose that Plato set out to show was not possible. There is no actual city in which all crimes done within it are adequately punished or all good deeds rewarded. The modern secularist, who has spent over a half century making movies of Hitler, must in the end admit that the gentleman's crimes really went without punishment. We Christians do not necessarily know what happened, but *Spe Salvi* does not belong to that theological school that maintains dogmatically that everyone is saved. The Pope says that even if through repentance the man who kills another is saved, there will still be distinctions in Hell.

So, I look on Hell as a kind of liberal doctrine. It says straightforwardly that our acts are of transcendent importance. We do not trifle with one another about ultimate things. We do not escape from our crimes even if we do so in this world. Not everything is forgiven if no repentance is forthcoming. Much of this is already in Plato. Indeed, there is a wonderful passage in the *Phaedo* in which the punishment of the unjust is being described.

It seems that those who have committed great crimes are cast into the river to be circulated about Tartarus endlessly until—and this is significant for us Christians—the person against whom we committed the crime forgives us. We have an advocate, that is Christ the Lord, but it is the same principle. You see why I like Plato. And why I take with a grain of salt all those pundits who are so horrified by the doctrine of Hell. If they had their way, our lives would be totally meaningless.

Q. #8): (CO) Can you leave us with one of you famous lists? Perhaps: "A List of books that you should have read by the time you are eighty."

A. #8): (JVS) Carl, it may be immoral to give Schall temptations he cannot resist! Before I do, I want to say that often I have said that on the day I die, I hope my shelves contain many books that I intended to read but never got around to. Why do I say this? Simply because no human being should delude himself that he has read it all. I know many friends and scholars and ordinary folks who are far more well-read than I. I have often had the experience, somehow I think of Scott Walter or Andrea Ciliotta Rubery, of suggesting a book, a book that took me days and weeks, even months to read. Two days later, not only do they tell me what the book was about, but they want to know if I have any other suggestions.

Just today, I received an email from a student who had been in my class a couple of years ago. He confessed to me that he had not read carefully all the books that I had assigned in class, but now with a little experience—he tells me he is a stand-up comedian in New York!—he realizes that he missed things that would be useful and important to him now after a little experience. This is just what Plato said to young men in book 7 of the *Republic*. He wanted to know if I had any books I might suggest to him! Well, I did.

I told him to look up the lists in *Another Sort of Learning* but in particular to read James Thurber's *My Life and Hard Times* and Chesterton's *Orthodoxy*. But here is your requested list:

TWENTY BOOKS TO BE READ BY THE TIME YOU ARE EIGHTY

1) Chesterton, *Orthodoxy*
2) Schumacher, *A Guide for the Perplexed*
3) Kreeft, *The Philosophy of Tolkien*
4) Lewis, *Till We Have Faces*
5) Pieper, *Josef Pieper—an Anthology*
6) Belloc, *The Four Men*
7) *Boswell's Life of Johnson*
8) Jane Austen, *Persuasion*
9) Simon, *A General Theory of Authority*
10) Guardini, *The Humanity of Christ*
11) Dawson, *Religion and the Rise of Western Culture*
12) Jaki, *The Road of Science and the Ways to God*
13) Sayers, *The Whimsical Christian*
14) Dostoyevski, *The Brothers Karamazov*
15) Huizenga, *Homo Ludens*
16) Morse, *Love and Economics*
17) Arkes, *First Things*
18) Derrick, *Liberal Education as if the Truth Really Matters*
19) Baring, *Lost Lectures*
20) Sokolowski. *The God of Faith and Reason*
Permit me one book of Schall: *On the Unseriousness of Human Affairs*.

Thanks for the questions, I enjoyed them.

Chapter 9

"Football was always the most dramatic sport. Basketball perhaps was the most artistic. Track the most individually oriented. The others sports depended on teams; but, like golf, track is more your own effort and responsibility."

Interview by Perry Bell, Sports Editor, Knoxville *Journal-Express* (PB) with James V. Schall, S.J. (JVS) on being inducted into the Knoxville High School Sports Hall of Fame*

Question #1): (PB) I see that you were born in Pocahontas—what brought you and your family to Knoxville?

Answer #1): (JVS) My father, Lawrence Schall, was the son of a farmer/banker. My father was one of eight siblings in a German/Irish family. My mother, Grace Shimon, was the daughter of a farmer/banker. She was the third from last of fourteen children, in a Bohemian family. My father went briefly to Creighton University when the farm crisis of the 1920s hit. After they were married, our family lived in Carroll, Dubuque, Pocahontas, and Eagle Grove before coming to Knoxville in 1935. I had two brothers—Jack, now deceased, and Jerry, and one sister, Norma Jean. My mother died in 1937. My paternal grandmother took care of me, my two brothers and sister. She died in 1942.

The following year, my father married Mary Fantz, a lovely widow with two daughters, Mary Jo and Jeanne Louise, who were in my class in high school. We graduated from KHS in 1945. Mary was from Missouri, a dental hygienist at the Veterans Hospital. We moved to a large Bellamy home on the corner of Robinson and something, I forget. My father managed the Gamble Store in Knoxville, which was located on the square, next to Penny's at the time.

* Perry Bell, Interview with James V. Schall, S.J., in the Knoxville, Iowa, *Journal-Express*, February 19, 2014.

Q. #2: (PB) Tell me a little about your school days, playing football, basketball, and track. Which was your favorite sport? And Why?

A. #2: (JVS) My father and my uncles on my mother's side were evidently good basketball players. I remember Dad telling us that the average score was something like 7-6 in his day. This was because there was no ten-second rule, so the art of dribbling and keep-away was what the game was about. I remember the famous track meets between East and West Ward grammar schools when we were kids. This meet was a big deal. Junior high was what, grades five to eight? The principal Nell McGowan and the math teacher Mary Jones were memorable, but Miss Jones may have been in high school, anyhow she was good.

Football was always the most dramatic sport. Basketball perhaps was the most artistic, track the most individually oriented. The other sports depended on teams; but, like golf, track is more your own effort and responsibility. In the conference we were in, called South Central in my day, we were pretty well matched with surrounding towns—Indianola, Chariton, Albia, Pella, Winterset. When we played Oskaloosa, Dowling, or Newton, we knew we were in for a beating. We figured if we put up a good fight, it was a sort of moral victory.

Q. #3): (PB) What was your best leap in the pole vault? What was your winning height in 1944 Drake Relays? Did you compete in 1945?

A. #3): (JVS) The height was ten feet, nine inches, about half of today's records. That was with the old bamboo poles. These were rare during the war years. I did compete the following year but by that time there were some pretty good vaulters from other towns who soared above me. It has been interesting to watch the evolution of this sport. All sports are affected by technology in various ways. The development of the flexible fiberglass poles transformed the sport, as did the emphasis on shoulders as much as speed.

Q. #4): (PB) I see you mention Omar Ray and Vance Wymore. Who coached you in each sport? In my research I have learned a little about both men. How would you describe them? What made them good coaches?

A. #4): (JVS) As I recall, when a man was hired as head coach, he was head coach for every sport. I forget why Coach Ray left KHS, probably he had a good offer someplace else. I believe in those days, coaches had also to teach; they probably still do. We had another coach, Carl Specht, who did the freshman/sophomore teams, as I recall. First of all, these were good men. They were demanding in a way that made you want to play for them. Also they knew how to win. My time was dominated by players like Dude Williams, Bob Mark, the Voyces, the McConvilles, Larry Mischler and Myron May, the centers, any number of good linemen—Lee Hayes, Vinton Rowley, Ken McKay, Bob Nichols, and Bob Leakey.

Though I played basketball, I was not as adept as Beryl Hall, Bob Mark, and others. But the old Memorial Hall has many memories. And we were especially proud of the stadium out by the water tower and swimming pool. Knoxville High has been relocated and rebuilt several times since my day. The English writer Hilaire Belloc said somewhere that, if you want to preserve something, even a building, you better write about it. I did not know that at the time, but I see it is true.

Q. #5): (PB) How would you describe yourself as an athlete—height, weight, fast, slows, strong...."

A. #5): (JVS) In high school, I weighed about 145 as a sophomore and 165 as a senior about five ten or eleven. I ran sprints on the track team and was relatively fast for those days and in our league. I do remember, however, later going to the University of Santa Clara and running the 100-yard dash in the Modesto Relays, a prestigious meet at the time. At the end of the race, I could hardly see the winner he was so far ahead of me. Actually, my father did a lot of coaching for the pole vault. My one strength was speed, so that enabled me go as high as I did.

One other advantage that classmates of mine and myself had at this time was that anyone older was in the military. When the soldiers began to return, the whole competitive scene changed. But in high school, we had a good track team, pretty well-rounded for our conference—Dick McConville and R. G. Wolf were excellent in the hurdles. Track is a spring sport. Somehow, Knoxville did not have a baseball team in those days. That was in the hands of amateur leagues, as I recall. I played some baseball, and I liked the game, but never learned to hit a curve. Today, I suppose, there are baseball, lacrosse, and soccer teams, if not rugby.

Q. #6): (PB) After you left Knoxville, what path did you take to your present residence in Los Gatos?

A. #6): (JVS) When Jeanne, Jo, and I graduated from KHS, it was May, 1945. My parents had decided to move to San Jose, California, partly for college for us. The war ended that summer, with the bomb. I still remember the celebration in San Jose. I attended Santa Clara that fall, but joined the army for eighteen months. That took me to Fort Lewis, Fort Belvoir, and Camp Kilmer, and back to Santa Clara for the scholastic year of 1947–48. I had been on the post football team at Fort Belvoir and was on the freshman team at Santa Clara the fall of '47. That was the team that went on to win the Sugar Bowl in their senior year.

But by that time I had joined the Society of Jesus at Los Gatos. I studied later at Gonzaga University, and did my doctoral work at Georgetown University where I graduated in 1960. After that I returned to four years of theological studies in California, when I was ordained to the priesthood. In 1964–65, I spent a year of studies in Belgium and in 1965 was assigned to teach at the Gregorian University in Rome. Beginning in 1969, I taught one semester in Rome and one at the University of San Francisco. In 1978, I joined the Government Department Faculty at Georgetown, where I remained until I retired in December 2012. My "Last Lecture" can be found on You Tube.* It was then that I returned here to Los Gatos, which is a very lovely place, I must say.

Q. #7): (PB) I see you have written some 35 books, many on religious topics."

A. #7: (JVS) My doctorate is in political philosophy. A good number of my books—*At the Limits of Political Philosophy, The Modern Age*—are in that general field. I have a number of books on teaching and learning—*Another Sort of Learning, The Life of the Mind*—and some on individual writers or topics—*Reasonable Pleasures, Schall on Chesterton*. I like very much to do books of essays—*Idylls &Rambles, On the Unseriousness of Human Affairs*, and the forthcoming *The Classical Moment*.

I am not exactly sure you would call any of my books "religious." They usually have a bit of everything in them. My first book in 1968 was called *Redeeming the Time*, a book in 2006 was entitled *The Sum Total of Human Happiness*, and one in 2007 was called *The Order of Things*. The most recent book was called *Political Philosophy & Revelation*. The one with the oddest title is what I call my English book, as it was published there, *The Praise of "Sons of Bitches*,*"* which is to have an American edition shortly. So, we cover the waterfront.

---

* See You Tube "last lecture"/Georgetown/schall.

Q. #8): (PB) You are a priest, is that correct?

A. #8): (JVS) Yes, I am a priest, a member of the Society of Jesus, a religious order devoted to teaching. Universities like Boston College, Georgetown, St. Louis, Creighton, and many others are from this tradition. In Knoxville, early on we lived a few houses from the old St. Anthony's Church on Marion Street. I have seen the newer church out by the race track. This area was the fairgrounds in my day. The new church is very nice. I remember Father Garrity and Father Horan, good men. I had the pleasure of delivering a lecture a couple of years ago at St. Ambrose University in Davenport. Knoxville is in the Davenport Diocese. I had never seen its fine campus in my Iowa days.

Q. #9): (PB) Are you retired? You missed the ceremony, and I heard that you were lecturing.

A. #9): (JVS) I am retired, and I regret that I missed the dinner and awards ceremony. I was frankly leery about travelling in the snow. From what we read here, this year was definitely not the year to be travelling in the Midwest in the winter. I did give a lecture in New Orleans, so I still am active when invited. I am giving a lecture in Providence next week. I do quite a number of columns and essays for various websites and journals, to keep busy.

Q. #10): (PB) Anything else pertinent to this story?

A. #10): (JVS) First, let me thank you for inviting me and for this interview. It gives me a chance to think of Knoxville again. I do not know if I have any KHS classmates still alive in Knoxville. The only one I know is Shirley Johnson Bellamy. Myron May is still alive in California. My sister Mary Jo lives in Utah. I am sure there are others but I do not think they live in Knoxville.

One thing I would say, in retrospect, is that it was a nice thing to have gone to a small high school in which, because of its size, everyone could participate in something—sports, newspapers, plays, music. In larger schools, it is rare for one person to play football, basketball, baseball, track, and soccer. There is something nice in being able to participate in all of these sports instead of specializing in one. You did not have to be very good in any of them to play in all of them. Nor do you have to come from a big city to figure out the important things in life. They are right there before your eyes, if you just see them.

Chapter 10

"Often people just assume that everything will turn out all right no matter what they do. But it can hardly be like that. Plato's basic problem has always haunted me, ever since I was able coherently to formulate it. That is: 'Is the world created in injustice?'"

Interview by Danny Funt, Editor of *The Hoya* (DF) with James V. Schall, S.J. (JVS)*

Question #1): (DF) What led you to make this your last semester of teaching?

Answer #1): (JVS) Not any one thing, of course. In a broad sense, the day comes for everyone when he must decide. Just when is the best time is prudential, a judgment. I have had a number of annoying health problems in recent years. I do not want to begin a semester that I cannot anticipate finishing. It seems fair to the Department to give them time to find a replacement. Jesuit superiors give good advice here. But it is not rocket science. What Socrates, Cicero, and Scripture say on old age, as my students know, I take to be basically true. You make a decision and live with it. Many of my colleagues, just older than I, were required by law to retire at seventy. But now we are almost the only country in the world that does not discriminate against age. I will be eighty-five in January. Thus, I have been able to teach fifteen extra years, as it were. So it seems fitting to retire at this time.

Q, #2): (DF) Do you have plans after you depart in March?

A. #2): (JVS) Aside from the famous aphorism—"The best laid plans of mice and men..."—I will reside in the Jesuit House in Los Gatos, California, on the Bay-side slope of the Santa Cruz Mountains. This is the

---

* Interview in *The Hoya*, Georgetown University, December 2, 2012.

large center in which I first entered the Order in 1948. I spent my first years from the time I was twenty to twenty-four there. It serves now as an infirmary, a residence, and the offices of the Provincial of the West Coast Jesuit Province. A priest as priest does not "retire," even if he is officially retired. I have a number of writing projects that I hope to continue once I am settled in. I have family in California and old friends. It is not forbidden for stray former students to visit the place should they find themselves in the vicinity.

Q. #3): (DF) What is it about Georgetown that has kept you here for so many years?

A. #3): (JVS) Well, number one, I never had a better offer! Why would I want to go anyplace else? I have always had interesting and excellent students here. My colleagues in the Government Department have been good scholars and colleagues. The Jesuit community has been a place where I could study and write at my "leisure," to use Pieper's famous Aristotelian word. Likewise, Georgetown is in Washington. I have found any number of extremely intelligent and effective men and women who are friends and guides over the years. Washington is larger than Georgetown, but still Georgetown is quite obviously at home here also, though there is always the question of how much we can be or are allowed to be "at home" anywhere in this world. This unwelcome for Catholics is becoming more and more an issue, alas.

Q. #4): (DF) What are some of your fondest memories of Georgetown?

A. #4): (JVS) Amusingly, one of my fond memories was on the plane from California on which I flew to take up teaching here. I was on United or some airline that had one of those company magazines. The magazine that was in my seat had an article about the ten most "drinking" universities in the country. Lo and behold, Georgetown made this "exclusive" list of ten! That must have been in late 1977. I confess that I have not seen any current list, but I was always amused by that article. I have not myself observed much of this drinking here, but I know that it can be more of a problem than it should be. We all should know, as it were, how to drink.

As I often mention, the beauty of the Healy Building, in the morning sun, in snow, in fog, in Spring flowers against its base, or seen from Thirty-fifth street just before Visitation or from Key Bridge, is not easily to be forgotten. Los Gatos has its own beauty, as most places do. When I taught in Rome or San Francisco, I was ever struck by beautiful places and vistas. But I think the campus is defined by the Healy Building and that is fixed in my memory.

But I suppose my fondest memories are those in a large class after I have finally succeeded in identifying each student by name and face, to see a student suddenly catch the drift of what Aristotle or Aquinas or Nietzsche or Plato was talking about.

Q. #5: (DF) Is there some text or topic that you have found most interesting to teach?

A. #5: (JVS) The good thing about political philosophy is that it requires one to be open to everything, not just itself. I am more interested in texts, as it were, that open us to everything.

Each of the books that I assign in courses has a particular place within the whole not only of the course, but of the intellectual life itself. In my second course each semester, I have followed an eight-semester cycle. In the course of four years, a student will cover a semester on Aristotle, then Aquinas, on Plato, then Augustine, on classical theory, then medieval theory, natural law, then Roman Catholic Political Philosophy. My books *Another Sort of Learning*, *A Student's Guide to Liberal Learning*, *The Mind That Is Catholic*, and *The Life of the Mind* are designed to call to students' attention books and ideas that they are not otherwise likely to encounter.

Q. #6): (DF) What non-religious text have you studied the most? How many times would you estimate that you have read it?

A. #6): (JVS) I am not quite sure why a non-religious text has any superiority over one that is said to be religions. Is Augustine's *Confessions*, which I have read many, many times, a "religious" or a secular text? The division "secular/religious" is much too narrow. C. S. Lewis tells us that if we read a great book only once, we have not read it at all. Yet, I have conceived my task here at Georgetown to prod, incite, advise, and inspire students to work through certain essential texts the first time. What they will do next with them, I never know, really.

Lewis also tells us that after a professor has taught a class for many, many years, he will find that it is always new, if it is great. I have found that to be true. And having students enable such experience to happen even to unworthy professors. I have read or reread or looked over, say, *The Ethics* of Aristotle sixty or seventy times, probably more. I always remark to a class that it is always a new book. I continually find something insightful in it partly because my experience in the meantime alerts me to seeing things that I missed before, partly because I just did not understand something that becomes clear on further readings.

The texts that I suppose I ponder most are those concerning the death of Socrates. Whether these texts are or are not religious is open to discussion. Indeed, the same issue is brought up in the *Apology* itself. I suppose in some ways that I spend much of my time reading non-religious texts. But when one has done this reading, he comes across something like Benedict XVI's great encyclical, *Spe Salvi*, and it becomes clear that the whole modern world is little less than a spurious way of solving what most people would call a religious problem. My book, *The Modern Age,* is about this very issue.

But I do spend much time on Samuel Johnson. Is that non-religious reading? Rather it is everything that includes everything. One central thing that I always seek to teach is that philosophy is the knowledge of the whole. If we try to exclude religion, particularly Christianity, from the whole, which much of modern academia does attempt, we will just end up being unable to know the whole since we exclude from it what ultimately it is about.

Q. #7): (DF) In your personal studies of political philosophy, is there a topic that you still find confounding?

A. #7): (JVS) Well, far be it from Schall to say that there is nothing that he encounters that confounds him! That would be something of a divine claim. I have thought a lot about the mystery of evil, as we are wont to call it. Most of my political philosophy books discuss this issue. Often people just assume that everything will turn out all right no matter what they do. But it can hardly be like that. Plato's basic problem has always haunted me, ever since I was able coherently to formulate it. That is: "Is the world created in injustice?" It obviously seems to be unless we understand the lesson that is presented in the four eschatological myths in Plato. Josef Pieper's new little book, *The Platonic Myths,* for which I wrote an Introduction, seems to me to get at the heart of the matter.

Benedict XVI, himself a mind of truly superior intelligence and a careful student of Plato, never tires of reminding us that the one thing that

God will not touch is our freedom. Thus, it is always possible to reject what we are. Otherwise we would not be what we are. Much of political philosophy is a frantic effort to invent ways to avoid the consequences of our freedom and what it is for, namely that we reach the end for which we exist, but freely. On no other condition could it be ours. This too is why we need to read Augustine so carefully and so often. He understood both the darker side of our nature and its highest purposes better than almost any one of our kind.

Q. #8): (DF) What are the biggest changes that you have seen since you arrived here as a student?

A. #8): (JVS) Well, obviously, the campus has not really acquired much new land, especially anything close by. Hence, we have more buildings all over the place. Where I now live in Wolfington Hall was the back parking lot in my early years here, but before that it was a gully of some sort, I think. Georgetown remains a rather medium-sized school. Everything is now wired for sound and sight. What was once in paper is now on-line— announcements, grades, schedules, lectures, you name it.

I first came here in 1956 as a graduate student where I remained till 1960 when I finished my doctorate. Georgetown in those days had many great professors and I tried to take or audit each one of them. Often they were Europeans who came here one way or another because of World War II. I think of Heinrich Rommen, Goetz Briefs, Josef Solterer, Louis Dupré, Wilfred de San, Jan Karski, Rudolph Allers, Martin D'Arcy, S.J., Thomas McTigue, Karl Cerny, Valerie Earle, William O'Brien, Edmund Walsh, S.J., Jeane Kirkpatrick, Henry Veatch, Hadley Arkes, Evron Kirkpatrick, Howard Penniman, Carol Quigley, and any number of others. I suspect few of these names are known to today's students, even to the faculty. Yet many of them were giants and all were first-class.

Georgetown has long been known throughout the world, largely because of its law school, its medical school, the foreign service school, and the language school. The arrival of Patrick Ewing and John Thompson II put the school on the map in another way. No one should underestimate the fame that comes to a school through athletics, sometimes infamy, to be sure. Almost all the departments seem to have settled down to a good routine. No doubt the bureaucracy of the university, as elsewhere, is the most notable growth.

In a sense, there are three or four universities on the same campus. The university the students see, the university the faculty thinks it teaches in, the university the administration thinks it rules, and the university that is kept in physical shape by gardeners, drivers, cooks, craftsmen, and other service units, not the least of which is the one that keeps the computers going. The one that keeps the water flowing may in fact be of less importance.

Yet, a university is a place of the mind. The temptation of a place like Georgetown is politics. We are tempted to study politics before we pay much attention to either *what is* or *what man is*. I have been struck in recent years by how many of the basic names, dates, and places of our tradition students no longer know. Both the Bible and Shakespeare, not to mention Plato and Aristotle, Aquinas, and Augustine, are often but vague names. We have good courses on these sources, but in the clutter of general education, much of civilization is lost.

Q. #9): (DF) What about *The Hoya*?

A. #9): (JVS), Over the years, I have had some forty column/essays in *The Hoya*, plus a number of essays in other student journals. Probably one of the most influential essays I ever wrote first appeared in *The Hoya*, some years ago, called: "What a Student Owes His Teacher." This essay found its way into my book *Another Sort of Learning* and was, indeed, part of its inspiration. You would be surprised how many students have told me that the idea that they "owed" anything to teachers was new to them. Actually a number of my *Hoya* essays have made it into other Schall books. Over the years, *Hoya* editors would invite me to do a column. I always appreciated that courtesy.

These student essays were written as reminders of the higher things that liberal education should be about. Very often they arose from what we were reading in class. I have long been convinced that much of what a student encounters about what is important he must find for himself in books that no one seems to tell him about. If I receive a letter or email from a student, I usually try to give him back something short to read, sometimes a JVS *Hoya* essay or a *Schall on Chesterton* essay, but something that we both, student and myself, ought to think about.

Sometimes I think the imagery of what a university is, the "ivory towers," is not reflected on enough. The phrase is mostly said in derision, something similar to Plato's description in Book 6 of the *Republic* about why the philosopher has a bad name in the city. Modern pressure to make college a training ground for certain crafts or professions, as well as the demands of departments for more time for specialization, has left little time for reading and serious reflection. A student who spends twenty to fifty hours a week working on a ball team, volunteering, or goofing off simply misses what his time means here.

The university should be designed to protect us from the pressing world at least for a few years during which we are free to read and write and think. Even heavy class loads will interfere. Once a student leaves the Front Gates, he will be inundated with the world and the pressing problems of going forth to his life. The specter of the on-line university is no longer just over the horizon, the place where we only need a machine and an on-line connection. The essence of education is simple: a teacher, a student, a room, and a book. I often cite Yves Simon's remark that nothing can protect a young student from giving his soul to an unworthy professor. We have to seek the meaning of *what is*. This is the adventure that finally defines us.

Q. #10): (DF) Some people have criticized Georgetown for its failure to deal with its Jesuit and Catholic heritage? What is your view on this topic?

A. #10): (JVS) It is difficult to imagine what students know in much detail about Jesuits or Catholicism. I cannot tell you how many times people over the years have asked me whether Georgetown is still Catholic. Not a few students find this a very Catholic place. Others, I suppose, do not.

Q. #11): (DF) If you had one piece of advice to give to a freshman, what would it be?"

A. #11): (JVS) That is easy. Students have often heard Schall's basic advice: "Don't major in current events." Or as my older aphorism has it: "To be up-to-date is to be out-of-date."

Chapter 11

"The basic issue is the fidelity of the Church to what is handed down and to what is true."

Interview by Innocent Smith, O.P. (IS) with James V. Schall, S.J. (JVS)*

Question #1): (IS) In *Distinctiveness of Christianity* (Ignatius Press 1982) you wrote that one of the most pressing problems confronting the Church was an erosion of Christian intelligence, a failure to trust in reason's ability to reach truth and to understand truth in a manner consonant with Christian Revelation. What is the state of this problem two decades later? Have the efforts of Popes John Paul II and Benedict XVI to deal with this problem borne fruit in the academy or the wider culture?

Answer #1): (JVS) What is quite clear to me, as I have frequently said, is that Catholicism has never been intellectually stronger or culturally weaker. What is striking about the Catholic Church, especially under John Paul II and Benedict XVI, is that no political or academic leader in the world can match them either in general brilliance, dynamism, or, in the case of John Paul II, heroism. The papacy, clearly, has existed with mediocre and even bad popes. But it has not been doing this for the last century or more. What we are seeing, however, is a refusal, including among many Catholics, to come to grips with the force of Catholic intelligence.

The reason for this refusal, I think, is not primarily intellectual, but moral. In the post-Vatican years, especially, many took their cue about intelligence from one or other movements of modernity—at first Marxism, then ideological secularism, then simply conformity with a relativist culture. Once anyone has habituated himself to such views, once he has lived consciously the consequences of these views, his soul becomes closed to any

* Interview by Ignatius Smith, O.P. in *Dominicana*, on-line, September 9, 2011.

alternative. This is especially true if he is a cleric or an academic, I think. Almost the only thing that can arouse them, as David Walsh explained in his *After Ideology*, is finally seeing and suffering in the pain that the ideas themselves lead to. Not a few die unaware or unrepentant.

Christ's remark that the truth would make us free did not necessarily mean that we wanted the truth if it required the changing of our ways, especially if we have gained a reputation for views that are, at one point or another, against some basic principle of Catholicism. We often underestimate, I think, the allure of fame and the force of envy in our souls.

No doubt, as you suggest, the impact of these popes has been terrific. What we lack are equally learned bishops and priests. There is a Catholic lay intelligentsia that has established colleges, written important books, and developed websites that are often brilliant. The older established academic institutions have been relatively unaffected by papal movements or inspirations. They are in a kind of ghetto of academic correctness that will not consider the whole hypothesis on which modernity in effect is based.

Q. #2): (IS) Where could renewal of Christian intelligence arise? What role should religious orders, especially the Dominicans and Jesuits, play in such a renewal? What about Church universities?"

A. #2): (JVS) I think that I remain a Platonist or Augustinian here. It can only arise in the souls of young men and women who are moved or called out of themselves to consider *what is*, to consider the truth of things. John Paul II often spoke of the fate of the rich young man in the Gospels who, even having lived a good life, turned away from something higher. Ignatius of Loyola and Francis Xavier at the University of Paris saw the same thing. I suspect our Western culture is full of such "turn-aways."

Looking at Church history from the Middle Ages, we might assume that the vanguard of this reform of soul would come from such Orders. I am very pleased to see the intellectual activity in your province of the Dominicans. You Dominicans have never had many colleges or universities to speak of. But your *Studia* give you a certain freedom and independence to start anywhere there is an innovative initiative.

And I think an argument can be made that the presence on college campuses of a dynamic Order that is not just pastoral can make a difference. I am also, though cautiously, sympathetic with the on-line university efforts of the late Ralph McInerny as well as those of Fr. Joseph Fessio, S.J,

Professor Peter Redpath, and others. I do not think this avenue is a cure-all, but it may be a significant help. After all, on-line and on other sorts of things like Kindle and iPads we have access to much of what we need. I would add that Father Robert Spitzer, S. J.'s Magis Institute is of great innovative importance, as is Jennifer Roback Morse's Ruth Institute and Helen Hitchcock's Women for Faith and Family. Religious orders need at times renewals and are not, as such, guaranteed to last.

Sometimes, within universities themselves, promising attention to the Catholic mind can occur. Professor Thomas Smith and his colleagues at Villanova do well, as do the programs at the Universities of St. Thomas in St. Paul and Houston and what Anne Carson Daly does at Belmont Abbey College. I like what many of the smaller and newer colleges that do not hesitate to call themselves Catholic are doing. The best known are probably Christendom and the University of Dallas. Thomas Aquinas College in California is in a class by itself. It has done something quite unique in the history of Catholic higher studies. But there are a number of other innovations.

Notre Dame has a general studies program as does Rockhurst in Kansas City, with Professors Brendan Sweetman, Curtis Hancock, and their colleagues. But there is a lot of empty space. The School of Philosophy at the Catholic University of America has been the most important single source of intellectual life in the Church, but I would add that the Catholic University Press, Ignatius Press, and St. Augustine's Press have almost single-handedly kept before us the classical intellectual tradition of Catholicism

Programs, institutes, and schools have to be formed but they are never enough by themselves. We need a constant flow of well-prepared young scholars and sensible teachers. I have always been struck by the effect of one or two good teachers on whole generations. I think of Francis Slade at St. Francis College, Daniel Mahoney and Marc Guerra at Assumption, the whole School of Philosophy at the Catholic University of America, Russell Hittinger at the University of Tulsa, Raymond Dennehy at the University of San Francisco, Andrea Cilotta Rubery at SUNY Brockport, Joseph Hebert at St. Ambrose University in Davenport, James Hitchcock at St. Louis University, Brian Bemnestad at the University of Scranton, Douglas Kries at Gonzaga, Patrick Deneen at Notre Dame, Joshua Mitchell at Georgetown, Peter Lawler at Berry College, Mary Nichols at Baylor, Peter

Kreeft at Boston College, John Finnis and Gerard Bradley at Notre Dame, Joseph Pearce at Aquinas College, Randall Smith and John Hittinger at the University of St. Thomas in Houston, Jay Budziszewski at the University of Texas, Thomas Michaud at West Liberty University, Joseph Koterski, S.J. and Christopher Cullen, S.J. at Fordham, Elisabeth Abromitis at Loyola in Baltimore, Robert George at Princeton, Mary Ann Glendon at Harvard, and so many others. One needs to note the increasing influence among us of French scholars such as Rémi Brague and Pierre Manent.

I would note too that much of Catholic intelligence today is found outside the schools. Individuals like George Weigel, Michael Novak, Tom Bethel, Kenneth Masugi, Patrick Riley, Robert Royal, Mark Henrie, Gerald Rousello, the Kirk legacy at Piety Hill in Michigan, the Lumen Christi Institute in Chicago, Father C. J. McCluskey, George Marlin, Father George Rutler, Robert Reilly, Father Robert Sirico, Father Mark Pilon, and others take up many projects that would never arise in the universities or treat them in a way that is free of many academic prejudices. And there is life in some of the seminaries—Mt. St. Mary's, the Josephinum, St. Charles, St. Thomas in Denver, and St. Thomas in St. Paul, with Christendom, University of Dallas, Thomas More, Franciscan University of Steubenville. Certainly *First Things* has been a force. Many of the journals are now on-line.

Q. 3): (IS) How can one best present the truths of philosophy to a skeptical culture that rejects absolute truth claims?

A. 3): (JVS) Your key word is "best." Plato is filled with young and old men who have truth presented to them but, in the end, they reject it and walk away. The premise of your question is something like that: "If we could present 'the truth of philosophy' in the right way, the skeptics would turn to absolute truth." The skeptic's problem is not just intellectual, as I suggested earlier. Probably the two most successful writers to deal with this issue in recent times are C. S. Lewis and Chesterton. What they both did brilliantly, I think, was to take the premises of modern skepticism and relativism and carry them to their logical conclusions as in fact amusingly untenable. Probably the best at this type of polemic today is Hadley Arkes.

If we read much Augustine, we will be sure that people who reject absolute truth will always abound in most eras. We were never promised that the basic truths of philosophy would be accepted, even when they are well presented, perhaps especially when they are well presented. Plato said again and again that most people would look on philosophy as a waste of time or as foolish. Aristotle said that if we are brought up well, with virtue, we will see first principles more easily when we are old enough to grasp their meaning. He implied by this, I think, that if we are not well disposed to the truth, we will not accept it when it is presented to us. In this sense, Socrates' emphasis on ignorance as being the only cause of error needs to be modified so that there is a will component to our intellectual problems. We see where the logic of truth is leading us and we do not want to go there. So we turn aside to concoct some other theory to justify our actions.

Where does that leave us? We are only asked to pursue the truth, to stand for it, present it when we can. We are to be aware that it can well be rejected even if true. This concern does not mean that some ways are not better than others, some teachers or writers not more effective than others. But it does mean that every age will have its form of rejection of the truth.

Q. #4): (IS) Which author from Western tradition would be most effective in speaking to modern man about ancient wisdom? Whose thought would resonate particularly strongly in the modern mind and awaken it to those truths that have been forgotten?

A. #4): (JVS) Again, I wonder if we can assume that the modern mind will respond to any Christian initiative. We tend to think that the problem is with us. Unbelievers are just waiting for us to come up with the right formula and they will believe. It does not work this way. There is something in the modern mind that is not eager for the truth if the truth is indeed Christian, as it is. This is a hard saying, I suppose. It is written off as "arrogant" because, it is claimed, all things are relative. They aren't. We want to be ecumenical. We love "dialogue." The Church has never been more open to or prepared for dialogue. But no one really wants to dialogue if it means changing one's soul. They want us to agree with them that nothing can be true. On such dubious grounds, they consider us backward if we don't. Many of us are converted to this new relativist view, especially many Catholics in public and academic life. We underrate the power of "the world."

Still, to answer your question about those in our tradition, the principal book remains Augustine's *Confessions*. I have been rather taken with the *Apologies* of St. Justin Martyr, the first philosopher to become Christian. I have heard a bishop say that he thought his successors would spend much time in jail, martyred or underground in this country. All the elements of a legal and probably physical persecution are now in order. Justin makes good reading in this context. I also like Irenaeus of Lyons. We no longer are willing to talk of "heresies." He is. The culture wants us to agree that every religion is equal, that all say the same thing, that it does not matter what you think or hold, just so it is not the truth. Since the truth is the only thing worth holding, we are on a crash course. But many will fall away.

Q. #5): (IS) You have written that one of Christianity's major vocations is "to preserve the very possibility of the full growth of *Eros* (*Distinctiveness of Christianity*, 205)." You continue that this issue is central to Christianity's "eternal struggle against the Manicheans." How are the current political and cultural struggles over the family and marriage a part of that eternal struggle? How can we appropriate the strategies used by past Christians in the current debate?

A. #5): (JVS) Actually, this question flows from the previous one. Decades ago I wrote a book, *Human Dignity & Human Numbers*, in which I spelled out the logic of the undermining of *Eros*. We can roughly say that 90% if the disorders in society and the consequent problems with faith come from not understanding or not following what *Eros* is. The issue is called "Manichean" in the classical sense that separating body and soul, we could maintain that nothing we did with the body, as it were, made any difference to our soul. Thus, Manicheanism seemed like a charter of liberty. Once launched on this path, every logical step took us away from what *Eros* is.

The sequence is really amazingly logical and clear. We begin by separating intercourse and childbearing. Since intercourse has no intrinsic relation to children, it is for its own sake. When it is so separated, it need not be a relation of man and woman. If children accidentally result, they are not wanted and can be disposed of.

Since childbearing is not related to intercourse between a man and woman in a stable family for the good of the child, we can proceed to "beget" or produce children outside intercourse. Children become products not of *Eros,* but of scientific calculation. Science proposes that it can "improve" the breeding. It can also propose producing varieties of slaves with human and non-human genes. Children then become products of science, technology, and politics. Politics decides what "sort" of a child we want to bring forth. Not the child of John and Suzie, but the "perfect" child of designer genes. And since the child is really a product of science and state policy, the government will educate them in its own image. We take literally Plato's scheme in Book V of the *Republic*. We carry out C. S. Lewis's *Abolition of Man* and Huxley's *Brave New World* and hardly notice.

In this context, *Eros* is left as a kind of recreation. It has no lasting tendency to *Eros* itself. A product-less *Eros* is intrinsically frustrating. *Eros* loses its charms when it loses its purpose. Make no doubt of it, the only organization in the world today that defends and understands *Eros* is the Church, paradoxical as it sounds.

Q. #6): (IS) Do you see any signs of renewal in religious life in America? What are the key issues any renewal of religious life must face in our current culture? How can they best be met?

A. #6): (JVS) One curious sign is the number of vocations that are coming from immigrant groups—Filipinos, Vietnamese, Africans, Mexicans, and other Latinos. Of course, in Latin America itself the Pentecostals seem to be having a field day converting Catholics. On the other hand, there is an amazing, quiet conversion of Pentecostal and other Protestant ministers to Catholicism. Once Pentecostals realize they have to deal with reason, the Church is the real alternative. Their major roadblock is unbelieving Catholics.

Probably the most important single step to reform is the clarity with which the Church in seminaries and schools makes it clear that homosexuals are not to be ordained. Along with this concern is the full Christological reason why women are not ordained. It has nothing to do with "fairness" or "rights" but with the Incarnation and its relation to the distinction of the sexes as itself a good. Widespread confusion on this issue of who is to be ordained has kept many a seminary empty or sparsely populated. Once the clergy seems to approve this form of life, the normal way as indicated in the previous question will reject it. Marriage and priesthood go together in their separate ways. No real marriages, no future clergy. *Eros* and *agape* meet.

At present we are very close, through government policy, to having to close our schools and hospitals and other institutions over this issue. The effort to eliminate the Church on this basis is relentless on both the national and international scale. It is something rarely faced head-on. Ironically, the sex abuse scandals were, in fact, mostly over this issue, though that was not clear. The Church found itself caught in a dilemma: it had to pay the price for abuses rooted in homosexuality and at the same time not be accused of being against the new way of life. We allowed the issue to be framed as if it were primarily a "religious" question which, like the abortion issue, it is not.

It is sometimes said that "conservative" orders or dioceses are experiencing new life. It is a misnomer. The most radical events in our culture are conversions to orthodox Catholicism and vocations to a way of life that is neither liberal nor conservative or even measured by either term. It may mean a large-scale numerical decline of Catholics while souls are reoriented to a proper order. The basic issue is the fidelity of the Church to what is handed down and to what is true. Once that fidelity is put in doubt in a country, a diocese, or Order, as it would be by large-scale capitulation to the culture on these issues, no real Church will remain.

Q. #7): (IS) Popular narratives of contemporary Catholicism often pit a dying older "liberal" generation against a rising young "conservative" generation. But the struggles of the "JPII" generation of priests and the widespread departure of youth from the faith suggests that there are some problems with that story. What do you think the major struggles facing the Church are internally and externally? How can Catholics best confront them? What pitfalls must they avoid?

A. #7): (JVS) Several commentators, among them Robert Royal and Father Barrone, remarked on the press coverage of World Youth Day in Madrid. Here we had a million and a half young folks with nary a reference to it except in terms of Spanish politics or opposition to the Church. No other event in the world of that proportion could have taken place for any cause and been deliberately ignored. That is itself significant. The world chooses to ignore. A case can be made that this inattention is a good thing. Many things in fact happen in the Spirit that are not visible to the world.

On the flight to Spain, Pope Benedict remarked: "These World Youth Days are a sign, a cascade of light; they give visibility to the faith and to God's presence in the world, and thus create the courage to be believers. Believers often feel isolated in this world, almost lost. Here they see that they are not alone, that there is a great network of faith, a great community of believers in the world, that it is beautiful to live this universal friendship."

Benedict XVI is not a pessimist and he is certainly not blind. He knows the score, probably more than any other public figure of our time. He also told some young nuns in Madrid: "We see a certain 'eclipse of God' taking place, a kind of amnesia which, albeit not an outright rejection of Christianity, is nonetheless a denial of the treasure of our faith, a denial that could lead to the loss of our deepest identity. In a world of relativism and mediocrity, we need that radicalism to which your consecration, as a way of belonging to the God who is loved above all things, bears witness." It was in this talk that Benedict used the phrase "Gospel Radicalism," not "Gospel Liberalism" or "Gospel Conservatism."

What is most important for the Church is the appointment of courageous, intelligent, savvy, and believing bishops. My sense is that the Church has been a bit lopsided in recent decades with brilliant popes but too few bishops who similarly stand out. Of course, these same popes appoint the bishops, but I think it is becoming quite clear that this governing duty is the major task of the papacy. We are going to need courageous bishops in almost every diocese.

If we look around the world, to China, to the Muslim States, to India, to Europe itself, there are few places that are any longer open to any kind of free and open missionary work. Latin America is more a Protestant mission. People talk of a third-world Christianity. There may be something to it. I suspect that Pope Benedict thinks that the crucial struggle is over the soul of Europe. Belloc's famous "Europe is the faith" makes more sense when the popes worry about Europe's massive loss of faith.

The major "pitfall" to be avoided is, I think, that of not standing for, making clear, and defining the truth. The truths at issue are, curiously, often those of natural philosophy and not revelation. All recent popes have understood this, from *Humani Generis*, to *Pacem in Terris*, *Humanae Vitae*, *Fides et Ratio*, *Spe Salvi*, and the "Regensburg Lecture." Chesterton was quite right. It will be the Church who last defends reason and the proposition that the grass is green and the sky is blue, that men are men and women are women. It is simply not true that the Church has not understood and responded to the major intellectual disorders of our time. As I said in the beginning, intellectual understanding is also a function of how we live and how we want to live. The central issue in this sense is, ironically, "choice." We are back at Genesis, almost literally.

To conclude briefly, I would offer one piece of advice. Read Pope Benedict's *Jesus of Nazareth*. No reading can better give the grounds of what we are. It is quite clear in this book that the man we know as Jesus of Nazareth is what He said He was—the Son of God. As the pope says, once we understand that God actually was man in this world, actually was God, nothing will be the same, not even His rejection.

Thanks for these questions and for letting me think about them. They are opinions, to be sure. I am most pleased to hear of this publication of yours. I have written in the *Angelicum* and *New Blackfriars*. It is always an honor.

Chapter 12

"To teach is to make present to another what is true and how to see it by himself. Teachers do not own knowledge. It is free."

Interview by Sophia Mason (SM) with James V. Schall, S.J. (JVS)*

Question #1): (SM) What was the best course you ever taught? Answer #1): (JVS) As I taught every semester a course on the nature of political philosophy, that was probably my best course. I always found it a delight. I taught an eight-semester cycle that included the following semester courses: Plato, Augustine, Aristotle, Aquinas, Classical Political Philosophy, Medieval Political Philosophy, Natural Law, and Roman Catholic Political Philosophy. Each of these was an insightful, often wondrous course; probably the semester with Plato was the most memorable, though I liked them all. When one has finished a semester on Aristotle, Augustine, or Aquinas, he can hardly imagine how much he still has to learn from these great men.

Q. #2): (SM) What book of yours do you think was the most worth writing? Which others do you think will still be read in fifty years? A. #2): (JVS) Goodness, I should be pleased if any Schall book were read in five years. *Another Sort of Learning* is undoubtedly the book that has received most attention. I think *Roman Catholic Political Philosophy* is the one that solves the most theoretic problems. The book that I like best is *On the Unseriousness of Human Affairs*, but *The Praise of 'Sons of Bitches': On the Worship of God by Fallen Men*, and *Idylls and Rambles* are more autobiographical and are books that I have enjoyed doing. My best literary form, as it were, is the short essay. I do a regular column entitled "On Letters

---

* Interview with Sofia Mason, December 6, 2012. Later basis of article in *National Catholic Register.*

and Essays" in the *University Bookman*. I think Belloc was the greatest essayist in our language. I do love the short essay. In fact, the subtitle of *Idylls and Rambles* is precisely "Lighter Christian Essays." The *Schall on Chesterton* book is in this category, as is *Unexpected Meditations Late in the XXth Century*, and in the forthcoming *The Classical Moment*.

Q. #3): (SM) How do the roles of a priest and a teacher fit together? Does being a Jesuit have anything to do with it?

A. #3: (JVS) At least one of the purposes of the Society of Jesus was to combine the priest and teacher into one person. A priest simply knows things that a teacher is not likely to know. To teach is also one of the duties of the priest. St. Paul said that teaching is one of the possible manifestations of the variety within the Church. To teach is to make present to another what is true and how to see it by himself. Teachers do not own knowledge. It is free. One of my best essays was entitled "What a Student Owes His Teacher." Both teacher and student pursue the same thing, the truth itself. If they do not, both are lost.

Q. #4): (SM) You left the army to join the Jesuits. How did this come about? Is there any leftover army in you?

A. #4): (JVS) Well, I did not exactly leave the army to join the Jesuits. I had an eighteen-month enlistment after World War II. On finishing that, I went back to the University of Santa Clara. It was at the end of my first year there that I entered the Order. Do I still have any army left in me? Every time I make my bed in the morning, I thank God for the army. One of my best essays is in *The Mind That Is Catholic*—"The Real Alternative to Just War." It is about the need and rationale for need of a military. The first essay in my Maritain book—*Jacques Maritain: The Philosopher in the City*—entitled "Justice, Brains, and Strength," deals with this issue also. I must confess little patience with pacifists or those who are unwilling to see that sometimes the lack of strength and the will to use it reasonably is itself a cause of greater injustice and suffering than the use of force when needed.

Q. #5): (SM) Chesterton is frequently characterized as a brilliant but unsystematic thinker. Is that a fair characterization and (if the latter part is true) does the unsystematic nature of his writings pose any problems for studying him?

A. #5): (JVS) Chesterton, as you know, is simply the greatest. On the hundredth anniversary of the publication of *Orthodoxy*, I wrote a long essay on this book in *Telos Magazine*. *Orthodoxy* is simply the greatest book written in the twentieth century, and I have not seen a better one yet in the twenty-first. The major premise of the question about Chesterton being unsystematic is roughly that real thought only takes place in systems. Usually what takes place in systems is ideology. What Chesterton was is a metaphysician. He went where *what is* took him. That is why he understood St. Thomas practically without reading him. No more orderly mind ever existed than Chesterton except perhaps Aquinas. Neither one had a system.

The real problem in reading Chesterton, as a lady once asked him, is his humor. She thought that one had to be serious to be a philosopher. Chesterton told her, "Madam, the opposite of funny is not serious, the opposite of funny is not funny." There is absolutely no reason why truth cannot be found in humor or presented in a humorous way.

Why people have difficulty in reading or appreciating Chesterton, I think, has nothing to do with his supposed unsystematic mind. It has to do with his clear grasp of the truth and where arguments contrary to it lead us. The conclusion of his 1905 book, *Heretics*, always seems to me to state the real issue. Modern philosophy has separated us from *what is*. It now takes faith to affirm whether the grass is green. One cannot read Chesterton very long without examining his mind. He must be put away or put off by calling him unsystematic or funny to avoid the real implications of Chesterton, which is that Christianity has it right about man, the cosmos, and God. If we live our lives in a way that allows us to blind ourselves to his logic, we will have to find ways also to reject reality itself. This rejection, as I tried to point out in my book, *The Modern Age*, is what we are about today. But if we want to know what reality itself is about, we had best read Chesterton.

Chapter 13

"Probably the great fruit of Belloc's sense of history is the fact that the events that appear on the record of history are filled with human choices and indeed human sins."

Interview by Annamarie Adkins (AA) with James V. Schall, S.J. (JVS) on Belloc.*

Question #1): (AA) Could you explain something of who Hilaire Belloc was, and the times in which he wrote?

Answer #1): (JVS) Belloc died fifty years ago, in 1953. He was an Englishman, in that his mother was English, but his father was French and his wife was an American. One of his sons was killed in World War I, and a second in World War II. Belloc had attended Newman's Oratory school in Birmingham. He went to Oxford, and was a member of Parliament for a brief time. He was a man of all sorts—a sailor, a poet, an historian, a controversialist, a philosopher, a born Catholic. I think he was the finest essayist in the English language. Someone remarked that in reading his detailed historical and geographical writings, one would think that, to do so, he was born in every country in Europe since he knew them so well.

Q. #2): (AA) Belloc once stated that Europe is the Faith, and the Faith is Europe. What did he mean, and what relevance does that statement have today?

A. #2): (JVS) This is one of the most refuted statements in all historiography. There are those who purport to think that Europe came from every background but Christianity. The zeal with which the Holy See is pursuing its insistence that the new European Constitution contain a reference to Christianity seems to suggest Belloc was on track, in spite of the

---

* Interview in Zenit, October 10, 2003.

denials. The fact is that without Christianity, Europe is not Europe. In fact, with the rapid decline of its birthrates, with large-scale Muslim immigration, and with a secularized Euro-elite, it is rapidly becoming something else. What perhaps might have surprised Belloc, though I doubt it, is that many Europeans want to rid Europe of any reference to its Christian origins. What will take its place will be something less than Europe as Belloc knew it, something neither Christian nor human.

Q. #3): (AA) How can Belloc's discussion of Islam in his books *Great Heresies* and *The Crusades* shine new light on our current world affairs?

A. #3: (JVS) The accepted doctrine today is that Islam itself is not a problem. As such, Islam is said to have no relation to world events that result in the need for defense in the West. There are, however, something called terrorists who cause all the problems. Even though they have Muslim names and claim the legitimacy of what they do to be found in their religion, their origins are said to be elsewhere—where, no one is quite sure. Western ideology forbids it to take Islam's notion of itself seriously. Belloc understood that Islam has a defined theological outlook and goal. Everyone should be Muslim. Force was useful in this goal. Belloc expected, if it ever acquired power again, that Islam would take up right where it left off after its last great territorial conquests. He would not have been in the least surprised at 9/11. Nor would he be astonished to find out that the Christians in the West are quite unprepared to understand the zeal for religion and conquest that Islam had and has in its faith. Many of the Muslim leaders today both desire and see possible, on a world-wide scale, the return to aggressive and active proselytism

Q. #4): (AA) How can Belloc clarify what our social sciences may prevent us from understanding, particularly the spiritual forces for good or ill?

A. #4): (JVS) Belloc was quite clear that it was spiritual forces that ultimately moved the world. The social sciences never understand such sources and have to rely on a reductionist methodology that invariably excludes such forces as they cannot be measured by their methods. Belloc was an historian who did not think that history had to happen the way it did.

He knows how it did happen. He did not think the English Reformation needed to have happened or to have happened the way it did. History is not "determined." Probably the great fruit of Belloc's sense of history is the fact that the events that appear on the record of history are filled with human choices and indeed human sins. The effect of this approach is to make us attentive to the spiritual forces that cause men to act or not to act the way they do.

Q. #5): (AA) Belloc was famous for popularizing an economic vision known as "Distributism." Is the distributivist solution of well-distributed property a cure for the economic problems of today?

A. #5): (JVS) People like Wendell Berry and Allan Carlson speak in terms of property, work, and ownership in a way that Belloc did. Chesterton once remarked that the electric motor was a factor that fostered small enterprise. One suspects that the personal computer has developed this emphasis in a new, even more graphic manner. Perhaps Belloc's most famous book was *The Servile State*. He was probably wrong in seeing the corporation, not the state, as the major problem that would reduce the people to a kind of happy servitude wherein they were taken care of in exchange for allowing the state to define all the conditions of their lives. But he certainly understood that this "all-caring" atmosphere was the main character of the future. He thought, with Dostoevsky, that men would give up their freedom in exchange for bread, or better in exchange for comfort.

Q. #6): (AA) One of Belloc's concerns was to invigorate a Catholic culture that would help overcome the loss of traditions common in a modern industrial society. Are any of his recommendations in this area valid today?

A. #6): (JVS) Things of truth do not become valid or invalid because of the time in which they are enunciated. A thing true on Monday, as Chesterton said, does not become untrue on Tuesday. Belloc's main concern about the Catholic culture was that it remain itself. This system of principle, insight, and truth was what alone could invigorate a culture. The real problem is not the "adaptation" of Catholicism to modern culture, but the judgment of modern culture by a Catholicism that remains itself, that remains what was handed down to it to keep present in the world.

Q. #7): (AA) Belloc has been criticized for his inclination toward an authoritarian style of politics and for his criticism of some groups of Jews. How can we adapt his writings to avoid some of these tendencies that were a product of the times in which he wrote?

A. #7): (JVS), If it is not possible to criticize "some groups of Jews" or anyone else for controvertible opinions, it is not possible to have a free society. We can only adapt his writings to avoid some of these tendencies that were a product of the times in which he wrote if we assume that truth is pretty much relative to time. The better approach is to face the issues as issues and try to understand the point Belloc was making. His book on the Jews was an attempt to point out that the Jews should be allowed to be Jews with their own homeland. What would have probably surprised him was the number of Jews who did not seem to want to return to the Jewish homeland. He assumed that the principle of "Europe is the faith" also applied, analogously, to a Jewish nation.

Q. #8): (AA) What is Belloc's legacy?*

A. #8): (JVS) Two of Belloc's most provocative statements are: 1) that the greatest spiritual invention is the twenty-minute Mass, and 2) that as we get older, we worry about the human structure of the supernatural Church. In both cases, he was being both amusing and incisive. That the main concern today is precisely the human side of the supernatural Church seems almost prophetic. If Belloc thought that Islam would rise again, it is probably only because he thought large numbers of Christians would be unfaithful to themselves and that Europeans would reject their heritage.

Nonetheless, the great legacy of Belloc is his essays. He wrote, and wrote well, of just about everything under the sun, everything on land or sea. He was jovial and solemn, funny and philosophical, ribald and pious, a man of the world and a man of home. Our kind has produced few, if any, like him.

---

* See James V. Schall, *Remembering Belloc* (South Bend: St. Augustine's Press, 2013).

Chapter 14

"When I say that reason leaves us with a certain longing, this refers to the basic truth that our minds are finite. We can never exhaust anything we know, however tiny or insignificant. All loves lead us to what is beyond our love. All knowledge leads us to what is beyond what we know from what is before us."

Interview by Edward Jones (EJ) with James V. Schall, S.J. (JVS) at Belmont Abbey College.*

Question #1): (EJ) How often have you visited Belmont Abbey College? Answer #1): (JVS) I have been to the College twice. The first time was a couple of years ago when Roger Scruton spoke. I had the pleasure of staying in the Abbey both times, and later of visiting with the Lindsley family in Charlotte; their daughter is now a freshman at BAC. The second time was in September when I was invited to give a Saturday morning lecture at which students actually showed up at a relatively early hour! They were a very good audience.

Q. #2): (EJ) As you have visited many colleges, what can Belmont Abbey learn from us and we from them?

A. #2): (JVS) The first thing would be not to worry too much about what others think if you are doing what you want to do and you have your own distinctive approach and character. Academia is full of "comparisons," usually odious, and "rankings" that tend to obscure the importance of distinctiveness. If survey after survey tells us that most people learn very little in college, the only lesson to be learned is not to do what everyone else is doing. But that takes courage. One seldom thinks of courage as an "intellectual" virtue, but it certainly is the most needed one today if truth is ever again to become central to academia's purpose.

---

* Interview published in *Crossroads*, Belmont Abbey College, 2010.

Q. #3): (EJ) You have lived and worked at a "dangerous crossroads" for decades now: the intersection where politics and religion meet. What are, say, the top 3-5 lessons you have learned from living and working at this crossroads?

A. #3): (JVS) Actually, ever since I finished my studies I have lived in the middle of Rome, San Francisco, or Washington. The first lesson is that religion and politics do not very often really "meet." The second is that every day modern politics looks more and more like a pseudo-religion. The third is that, as I like to put it, the Catholic Church, for its part, has never been intellectually stronger or culturally weaker. The people who do not know this are mainly themselves academics.

Q. #4): (EJ) With regard to your lecture at the Abbey ("Books That Are 'Great'; Books That Are 'True'"), let me ask you about your contention that someone could go to any university, great or small, famous or unknown, read all the books assigned and listen to the professors and "still never come close to inciting that drive to know *what is* that lies at the heart of our personal existence."

A. #4): (JVS) Some institutions have "Great Books" programs. It is a sort of uppity criterion. The Catholic tradition is not, as such, a Great Books tradition but a "pursuit of truth" tradition. The varying Great Books as such usually end up contradicting each other and confusing the readers, especially young readers, though not them alone! This fact does not mean that they need not be read. It means that you have to have some philosophic insight or intelligence as you read them. It is not only truth and good that have moved the world, but also falsity and evil, though these latter never unless they were also seen as somehow good. That is a good doctrine of Aquinas.

Q. #5): (EJ) That phrase *what is* seems to be fraught with meaning. It is one that recurs in many places in your work. Could you describe what comes to your mind when you use this phrase—and what perhaps should come to our readers' minds?

A. #5): (JVS) I suppose if you read Plato, Aristotle, and Aquinas enough, you will find yourself using this phrase. Everything that we encounter is a "what" that "is." There are a lot of "whats" that are not immediately before us. We even can imagine "whats" that do not exist except in the mind. But we cannot think "nothing" or "what does not exist" unless we first encounter then think *what is*. So this is the great defense of the world that is before us but one we did not make.

We keep reminding ourselves that, as Aquinas said, "Truth is the conformity of the mind with *what is.*" We are but small creatures, and we pursue truth and goodness through our encounters with *what is*, particularly with other persons of our kind who are. Behind this are the flashing words of Exodus, the "I Am" words that define the Godhead. The world is not an illusion. There it is, right before us, standing outside of nothing. We can only be astonished at its being there before us. That, I think, is what should also come before any reader's mind, namely, that things really are. We did not make them. We know that we did not.

Q. #6): (EJ) In your lecture, you also remark: "I think that the country and the world are full of people who realize that they really did not learn many of the important things as a result of their formal education." I do not think that knowing, or better, learning to know, is painless. What I do think, however, is that once we realize that "things exist and we can know them," to use Gilson's memorable phrase, we are on our way.

A. #6): (JVS) There are two parts of that remark. The first has to do with the growing recognition that we sense in our souls that what we were formally taught did not even begin to account for reality that is actually there before us. So many things were left out, deliberately so, usually. Most modern education does not allow us really to read and confront those human and divine lessons that will explain what we really are and what is our actual purpose and destiny. What I have sought to do is to address this sense that anyone can suddenly realize about what he knows and does not know. My many book lists are designed precisely for such souls.

The second part has to do with whether learning is "painless." The basic things generally require struggle and determination. I am not free to use grammar or Chinese until I have gone through the pains of learning them enough to use them without having to worry about how I am using them. I cited Gilson's phrase because we can suddenly see this principle operating in our own souls. That is, we realize that we can know a truth, that some things really are wrong or false. Knowing this, we can begin. If we begin by thinking that nothing is true, or can be true, that it is true that nothing is true. Then, we not only begin contradicting ourselves, but we have to admit that on such a basis nothing is worth knowing anyhow. If nothing it true, it makes no difference what we do.

Q. #7): (EJ) The word "things" also appears to be packed with meaning as it is used in that Gilson passage and elsewhere in your work. Could you unpack what you mean by that word a little for our readers as well? That is, are you touching on what your brother Jesuit Gerard Manley Hopkins was hinting at when he wrote: "There is the dearest freshness deep down things"? "Dappled things"?

A. #7): (JVS) Hopkins was said to have had Scotist leanings, but yes, things. *All that is,* is one, true, good, beautiful, and a not-that. Technically, the word thing refers to the whatness of something. This thing is a rabbit. That thing is a chair. The *what is* issue has to do with whether the chair or the rabbit exists or not. The thing question has to do with what it is. Joseph Pieper says that each existing thing has a two-way street about it. On the one hand, it need not be.

On the other hand, it is. All things but God have existences limited by their what, their form. They act in the way their form limits them. A dog acts in a dog way. The great mystery is not why there are so few things, but why so many. Our God is a God of superabundance. Each thing is of itself a nothing. It did not call itself into existence. On the other hand it is a something whose existence and whatness can never be exhausted since its very being is rooted in the Godhead. This is why there is nothing that is not fascinating.

Q. #8): (EJ) In your talk, you zeroed in on what some would say is the central problem of modern higher education, Catholic or otherwise: the seeming inability to teach/impart/inculcate wisdom, eloquence, judgment about what is good, true, and beautiful versus what is not. As you've put it elsewhere, students graduate knowing the names of "thinkers," but they do not themselves know how to think.

A. #8): (JVS) Much of this has to do with the level of virtuous (in the Aristotelian sense) or moral life among students and those just out of school. We cannot avoid facing the fact that an irregular moral life, personal life, will make us unable to see the truth. Why? Because we will spend out mind's energy looking for reason to justify what we do. Jennifer Roback Morse's book *Smart Sex* is very good on this issue, as is Aristotle himself. This does not necessarily mean that if we live a good life we will be "smart." but it does mean that if we do not, we will not use our minds on the proper object of *what is.* Knowing who said what is quite a useful and important talent. But it is not itself thinking. Thinking always means deciding, judging about the truth of what someone maintains. That capacity is the result of actually philosophizing and not just reading and analyzing a text.

Q. #9): (EJ) At "Schall's ideal college," how would the problem be solved? Or, if you prefer, what would "Schall's ideal college" be like?

A. #9): (JVS) First, it would not be run by Schall. Ralph McInerny recently remarked on the notion of making "research" the focus of university life. The "undergraduate research institution" is perhaps the greatest monstrosity ever concocted by the academic mind.

You cannot "re-search" until you have searched. The research concept is based on the idea that everything that we must know is in the future, on the idea that all that is studied today will be obsolete tomorrow. I constantly admonish my students not to "major" in current events. What was apparently important when one enters college, in that view, will be unimportant four years later.

The sheer amount of things that can be known is simply overwhelming. I suppose it always was and always will be. One hates to think that perhaps the world should have fewer things in it than it has, just so we could feel less overwhelmed. Of course, if the world had fewer things in it, it is possible that we would be one of them! The very essence of Socratic philosophy is to know that we do not know everything about anything. But this is not an admonition of despair. It rather suggests a transcendent purpose to our being.

Professor Thomas Martin at the University of Nebraska at Kearney has remarked that "A good university can be known only by her students who have gone into the world." I presume a bad university can be learned in the same way. Rather like Plato's "city in speech," my ideal university does not exist except in the minds of those who have attended it. It really is no existing institution. It is rather some books and some essays and lectures that suddenly wake us up. We can present really important material to students and they remain uninterested and clueless. What counts is the Platonic "turning around," and seeing in their own souls that there is something to know and that they would like to know it. Until this happens, it does not much matter what sort of university we choose to attend.

Q. #10): (EJ) Toward the end of your lecture, you cited the essay of Frederick Wilhelmsen, "Great Books: Enemies of Wisdom?" He said that the American Catholic academy once stressed philosophy, not great books which usually lead to confusion. In your estimate, what made the Catholic education system, as Wilhelmsen described it, superior?

A. #10): (JVS) Simply because it was based on the fact that there were things that could be known by philosophic teaching and reflection that are available to anyone with a reason. The history of philosophy is not philosophy, but, as Strauss once said, a collection of "brilliant errors." I have always been someone to take students to books, but to books that themselves teach one to think, even without a professor present. Good teachers and good students ponder the same things. Professors do not own truth. It is free. And the shock of our existence is that anyone can find it, even someone living in the midst of much error. There is a current in the Aristotelian tradition, taken up by John Paul II in *Fides et Ratio* and Benedict in *Spe Salvi*, to the effect that anyone can come to a knowledge of the truth.

Also within the Christian tradition from Paul there is a sense that the "learned" are the ones who are most distant from truth. The conformism that we see in modern universities often make me think of Paul on this score, the foolishness of the wise. Benedict remarked that the philosophy professor is not necessarily someone who actually pursues wisdom. I think that Wilhelmsen thought that philosophy could be learned by dialectic and reflection. It was not convertible with knowing its history, however valuable that was. The question is not what did Kant think of evil but Aquinas' question "*Quid sit malum?*" A university is where the basic questions are asked and answered. We have surprisingly few around. But not a few smaller Catholic and other institutions are getting the point.

Q. #11): (EJ) Given the rich inheritance Catholic colleges had/have to offer, why do you think they watered down or abandoned what made them unique in order to imitate the "elite" schools? (Joseph Bottum, the former editor of *First Things*, said in an interview in our last issue that it was because Catholic colleges had an "inferiority complex"—i.e., to put it somewhat crassly, a case of W.A.S. P. envy.

A. #11): (JVS) I was just reading an Aquinas commentary on the *Metaphysics* of Aristotle where he brought up the issue of envy. I have always remarked that envy is the most spiritual, and therefore, most dangerous of the normal vices. "Envy is sadness at someone's prosperity, which can only happen if the one who envies regards the good of the other as a diminution of his own good," is how Aquinas put it. Over the years, I have visited a fair number of Catholic colleges, old and new. They often have amazing plants in their own local area. They have become service schools and job training centers. This is partly the question of whether everyone should go to college or whether we should call every academic institution a "university," as we are now bent on doing.

Aristotle in a famous passage from book ten of his *Ethics* told us not to listen to those who tell us, being mortal, to think of mortal things or being human to think of human things. He suggested that to keep mortal and human things in place we needed first to attend to the divine things, however little of them we could know by the power of finite reason. No doubt, much of human life is taken up with human things, economic and political. Attending to such things is what we are. Christians in general have been stung ever since Marx claimed that they deflected man's interest to the next world and neglected this one. From *Rerum Novarum* on, we have been working to prove we knew just as much about the world as anyone else.

But what we have missed is something Benedict pointed out in *Spe Salvi*, namely that modern culture is itself shot through with an inner-worldly eschatology that is designed precisely to domesticate Christianity in this world. The older reaches of philosophy always ended up in a sense that this world could not and did not explain the essence of what we are ultimately intended to be. So, it was not just envy that was the problem. It was primarily theologians and philosophers who lost their faith in the real end of man. The schools simply provided *fora* for them. The recovery of the university involves the recovery of mind. That is something of the soul. "Inferiority complex" is a psychological term. I would tend to say that when we lose our faith we quickly lose our reason, but we retain a "ratiocination" that justifies this loss as if it were a good.

Q. #12): (EJ) At schools like Catholic University of America, Belmont Abbey College, and others, something that might be described as a "Great Reclamation Project" is going on. That is, we have a conscious attempt to bring back the glories of Catholic higher education, and to thus strengthen and renew our Catholic identity. However, the polarization between "liberal" and "conservative" Catholics and others in academia and elsewhere can make this difficult. How do we in Catholic higher education—liberal, conservative, or otherwise—transcend the current contentious environment and effect positive change?

A. #12): (JVS) I congratulate you Edward for asking me simple and easy to answer questions! One thing to do is pray that Benedict XVI lives as long as Leo XIII. He is the best mind of our time. Much can be done from the top. Indeed, the structure of the Church often seems providentially ordered that this might happen. The reason that the "Great Reclamation Project" has not proceeded further, I think, is that it is no longer mainly a Roman issue, except perhaps in the sense of good judgment on hierarchical appointees. The agenda is out there in public papal documents that are far ahead of anything coming out of the schools, more penetrating, more scholarly even.

I no longer think we can speak as if "liberal, conservative, and others" are neutral terms that indicate no fundamental difference in their conception of what Catholicism is. We cannot ask these groups just to stop bickering and get along. They do not agree on fundamentals. And there is always a *datur tertium*, something that is neither liberal nor conservative. Modern culture, as Tracey Rowland points out, is not neutral. Imitating it is not an indifferent act. It is putting oneself in a frame of mind and action that deviates from what is right or true in basic issues. The crucial area is, of course, the life area. Of all areas that is not neutral, this is tops. We are witnessing a concerted effort, legally and culturally, to make the practice of basic Christianity impossible. We are shooting for a Christianity that will conform. And many of our leading and most publicly known "leaders" are on the side of the culture, not the truth of the faith. We are blind if we do not see that.

Actually, I do not think traditional Catholic or religious institutions that have allowed themselves to be dominated by the culture can ever reform themselves. The most obvious thing is to begin new institutions, perhaps the on-line things of Father Spitzer or of Professor Peter Redpath is the way to go. The computer and the cell phone may be the next university campus, though I am not enthusiastic about it. But I can see that it might work for many. But bishops need to be bishops in the area of the academic life in their area. Unlike other countries, we have had a largely canon law episcopate and not a philosophic or theological one. But bishops need to be men of action. It is no accident that Benedict is an admirer of Augustine, not to mention Bonaventure.

Q. #13): (EJ) How do we continue to strengthen our Catholic identity in an uncompromising yet welcoming way (i.e., so that people from different faith backgrounds are not made to feel like "the other."

A. #13): (JVS) If I go to a Hindu or Muslim university, will their prime concern be about my "feelings"? I think that we should be what we are. If anyone wants to attend our institution, they do so on our, not their, terms. Why would a non-Catholic want to come to what is supposed to be a Catholic university and find that it is just like every place else?

The word "welcoming" has come to be too often a substitute for "relativism." At what point do we stop "welcoming" everyone? If all the commandments and the essentials of the natural law are in practice or explicitly denied, do we still "welcome" everyone? It strikes me that such tolerance theory has come to mean that there are no standards. No one wants to go to a place with no standards unless that is what they are looking for.

Q. #14) (EJ) Is part of the answer bringing a kind of Chestertonian playfulness to our work in education? If we Catholics have the "fullness of the Truth," why do we often seem to exude "the half-ness of the joy," both in the liturgy and in too many places in the academy? "Catholics don't celebrate their religion, they mourn it," as one wag put it. Or perhaps cultivate in the "madness of Christian intelligence" that you describe as the beginning of your new book, *The Mind That Is Catholic*?

A. #14): (JVS) It is often said that the one thing that a liberal cannot do is laugh at himself. I think Chesterton is the sanest man ever, but his playfulness requires a certain contentment with reality that is often lacking. Our problem is not only or principally ourselves. We cannot often enough grasp the fact that there are people, many people, who do not want to know the truth. We cover this over by suspecting that it is our fault. Catholics do not "celebrate" their religion; they celebrate the Mass. Religion is a natural thing; the Mass is from the Lord.

Christian intelligence appears mad because it is sane. It is the middle. It is the measure of how we ought to live and act and believe. The suspicion that such a position is true forces people not to accept it in advance since they know that it requires assent in the honest man. For the Greeks, it was not possible in a democracy to tell the difference between a fool and a wise man because they could not tell the difference. Christian madness is like this. To those who have disordered souls, it will appear as mad. It will also be the measure of truth.

Q. #15): (EJ) Some seem to have the perception that the Catholic mind is a closed mind; that to be faithfully Catholic is to be unquestioningly, submissively accepting of many "settled truths." To be Catholic you have to "check your brains at the door" is a frequently-leveled charge. "But we outside of your faith," some say, "are free to think for ourselves." However, in *The Mind That Is Catholic*, you write: "Reason at its best…leaves us with a certain longing, a certain unsettlement, an abiding intellectual search." What does the Catholic mind have to be unsettled about?

A. #15): (JVS) The Catholic mind is the least closed of any mind. It is a defect in the Catholic mind to neglect anything *that is*. It is more properly "Catholic" to question everything. Not to question at all is specifically un-Catholic. The whole structure of Aquinas is to teach us to question, but also to answer. The modern mind wants questions, but not answers. This latter is the root of its opposition to Catholicism. No Catholic has ever, to use your expression, ever checked his brains and remained a Catholic. The very proposition that we should do so is a denial of the essence of the Catholic mind.

When I say that reason leaves us with a certain longing, this refers to the basic truth that our minds are finite. We can never exhaust anything we know, however tiny or insignificant. All loves lead us to what is beyond our love. All knowledge leads us to what is beyond what we know from *what is* before us. "What does the Catholic mind have to be unsettled about?" The most famous line in all of Catholicism is probably that of Augustine, "Our hearts are restless until they rest in Thee." This is what we are unsettled about. We have not yet arrived in the City of God and we know it with every move of our being.

Q. #16): (EJ) You also write in your new book that "the Catholic mind is open to all things". Is it also "tolerant" of all things"?

A. #16): (JVS) It is open to *all that is*. To be tolerant of all things is to abdicate one's mind. To be tolerant of all things is a denial of any objective difference between good and evil. We may "tolerate" the sinner, provided that does not involve us in the affirmation that his sin is really a virtue. This is what the modern mind is often about, to affirm that what is wrong is right. We tolerated slavery for a long time. We no longer do so. We tolerated smoking for a long time. We no longer do so. We did not tolerate sodomy or divorce for a long time. We now do so. Toleration theory can be a practical or a theoretical thing. As a theoretical thing, it is little less than relativism that says that nothing is true. As a practical thing, we allow certain things lest we get something worse. That things can get worse while they seemingly are getting better is the definition of the modern age.

Q. #17): (EJ) There seems to be a certain restlessness or unsettlement among some educators of elite schools about their current model. Witness recent books like Harvard professor Harry Lewis's *Excellence Without a Soul: How a Great University Forgot Education*, or Anthony Kromman of Yale's *Education's End: Why Our Colleges and Universities Have Given Up on the Meaning of Life*.

A. #17): (JVS) Another cause is their cost. Universities routinely up their tuition. They all are bloated bureaucracies matched only by the federal and state governments. Actually, the real threat may be coming from the University of Phoenix and other on-line universities. But there is no doubt that universities all vote 90% the same way. There is really very little intellectual diversity in universities. They are closed shops, to borrow a union phrase. If you do not hire the right faculty from the right places, who publish in the right journals and presses, with the right recommendations, you are not a serious scholar. In the meantime, the pursuit of truth goes by the wayside.

The meaning of life is indeed about the last thing you will find really discussed in universities. And "excellence without a soul" is a pretty good way to put it. Allan Bloom said that our students have "flat souls." That is right. Nothing moves because nothing is true or serious. Lives are lived because there is no truth to measure them. The real mystery is not that some universities are restless, but why they all are not. The Catholic universities should be at the top of this list. But they are waiting to see what the mainliners do. 'Tis a pity, really.

Q. #18): (EJ) So might this not represent an opportune moment for colleges like Belmont Abbey to, in our own humble Benedictine way, fill a vacuum in American education? In short, shouldn't this be a time of great hope for a college like ours?

A. #18): (JVS) The Benedictine monks have been around for a long time. They go back to the very foundation of the West. They were, as I think Christopher Dawson said, the inheritors of the classic Greek city-state. No college will have a future unless it has a present. That present has to do with who is hired, what is taught, what is learned. Most universities have disordered curricula because their administrators and faculty have disordered souls. We should not forget that what is disordered can be immensely attractive. We can pine for the fleshpots of Egypt, but also for those of Harvard and Berkeley and Cambridge and the Sorbonne. I do not think that if a school is really teaching the truth that it will be "recognized." Truth is a lonely road. I am fond of saying that Catholicism has never been intellectually stronger but culturally weaker. But this weakness is self-imposed. There is nothing so difficult as intellectual courage.

No college like Belmont Abbey will fill the vacuum in American education. What it can do is to teach the truth to those who present themselves there. They will need to be charmed and directed. Catholicism has never despaired if it could reach a few souls who turned around to *what is*. This is why Belmont Abbey is important.

Q. #19): (EJ) Your remarkable output of books and essays shows a very fertile mind at work and a great work ethic, but also a terrific spirit of bonhomie. To what do you attribute your creativity, your productivity, and your sense of playfulness? Might it have something to do with the fact that you have always lived at the crossroads where reason and revelation intersect and that is a very potent "power source"?

A. #19): (JVS) Well, the religious life of a Jesuit was designed to give a man time and opportunity. He was left free to pursue what was true, if he would. This demanded a structure of religious life that encouraged large amounts of time and an atmosphere of scholarship and reflection. But it was also based on the idea that truth is to be communicated, presented.

I have had the good fortune to live in the very heart of three great cities for much of my academic life—Rome, San Francisco, and Washington. My earlier studies were in rather out-of-the-way places, but they were actually well designed to give a man the freedom he needed to figure things out, if he would.

Yes, I do think that there is a sense of delight and playfulness in reality. We are created for and in joy, no doubt of it. Chesterton, for whom I have the greatest admiration, was once accused of not being taken seriously because he was funny. He responded that the opposite of funny was not serious but "not funny." He saw no reason why truth was less truthful if it were presented in an amusing way than if presented in a solemn way. I would like to be as delightful as Chesterton or Boswell or Wodehouse. But I do find delight in things and I hope that comes across. We are created in and destined for joy, even the Cross.

Chapter 15

"As I like to put it, the universe does not look at us. We look at it. We seek to understand it. Moreover, the universe seems to betray an order that forms or checks the human knowing mind."

Interview by Christopher Hauser (CH) with James V. Schall, S.J. (JVS) in *The Dartmouth Apologia.**

Question #1): (CH) You have written and spoken many times about friendship and God. How do you define true friendship? How does this notion of friendship relate to the revelation of the Christian God as Trinity?

Answer #1): (JVS) It is always difficult to improve on Aristotle. Friendship differs from justice because it is reciprocal good will. We not only will the good of the other, but the other in turn wills our good. Benevolence means to will good to another, whether or not reciprocity occurs. Essential to this reciprocity is its mutual freedom, its lack of coercion. Friends not only will the good of the other, but will him the highest things, the things that are ultimately important. Friendships based on utility or pleasure may be perfectly decent and good. We cannot or do not want to get along without them. But they are limited to their object. The highest form of friendship is concerned with the exchange of what is really significant and important. Thus, it is also based in the truth.

The notion of friendship relates to God firstly because, in the books of revelation, Christ says specifically, "I have no longer called you servants, but friends." Our relation to God is not submission or subjection. For many philosophical and religious systems, this attribution of a friendship between

---

* Interview by Christopher Hauser with James V. Schall, S.J, in *The Dartmouth Apologia: A Journal of Christian Thought*, 7 (Fall 2012), 7–11.

God and man is a shocking notion. It is said to demean the Godhead. And Christians would agree that they themselves could never have imagined this relationship, had it not been revealed to them. This divine friendship was offered to them not by their own theories but by God revealing Himself. The idea never would have occurred to Christians on their own reasoning. But once revealed to them, they can think about just why the relationship might exist, might make sense with the understanding of God as revealed.

The essential answer begins with Aristotle's wonderment about whether his God was "lonely." The issue arises in the Tractate on Friendship. If friendship is seen by Aristotle, the philosopher, to be the highest external relation we can have with others, it seems that this relationship does not exist in God. Therefore, He seems lonely or defective. Once the inner nature of God is revealed as Trinity, as having within it an otherness of persons, Father, Son, and Spirit, it becomes clear that God does not necessarily lack within Himself what amounts to the love of another. Indeed, the definition of the inner life of the Godhead is a relationship of Persons to one another in which they exchange the highest things of their being.

If the inner life of the Godhead is itself a friendship, a love of one another for the sake of the other, it would seem to follow, at least as possible, that God could offer to free and rational persons a share in this inner life. It is not something that they could merit or earn simply by themselves. But it is possible that it be a gift to them. They can still individually reject receiving it. Not even divine friendship can be coerced. But the fact remains that it is not unreasonable to suppose that such a relationship might logically follow from a proper understanding of the inner life of the Godhead and the nature of friendship.

Q. #2): (CH) You spoke of the relationship of the doctrine of the Trinity to the philosophical question of "Why there is something, not nothing, or why is there a creation?" Here it seems that Christian revelation addresses itself to one of the foremost issues of philosophy, namely the question of creation. Can you explain this solution?

A. #2): (JVS) As Robert Spitzer, S.J., in his *New Cosmological Proofs for the Existence of God* and Msgr. Robert Sokolowski in his *God of Faith and Reason* have well said, the two issues should be separated. One is a metaphysical question of whether something can come from nothing. (It can't.)

The other is the state of contemporary science that seems more and more to acknowledge that the cosmos began some 13.7 billion years ago, that before it existed exactly nothing existed, yet everything seemed to come into existence in an orderly fashion. Indeed, many scientific facts seem to indicate that the cosmos itself has within it an anthropic principle, that is, it seems to be so designed that a rational being could exist within the cosmos.

Once we arrive at this position, which is also the Genesis position, the crucial question becomes: "What is the purpose in a universe of intelligence that is not itself divine?" It would seem that the universe itself is not complete unless it has within it an intelligence that can understand and appreciate it. As I like to put it, the universe does not look at us. We look at it. We seek to understand it. Moreover, the universe seems to betray an order (see my *The Order of Things*) that forms or checks the human knowing mind. That is, we seek to know *what is*, what is already there. We can check our mind, our theories, over against an intelligence that is found in things, a "substitute intelligence," as Charles N. R. McCoy called it in his great book, *The Structure of Political Thought*. In this sense, the intelligibility within the universe is meant to be discovered and known by the intelligent beings within the universe. But they are to know these things as part of or intrinsic to their own reaching the end for which they were personally and individually created.

This reflection brings me to your basic question, a good one. Some theories about the supposed lack of friendship in God suggested that God created the universe because He was lonely. He created it to find someone else to love. While such a position is wrong, we can see why it might be proposed. But if God in His Trinitarian life is complete, He needs nothing else. He is not lacking in friendship. Indeed, He need not create at all. God is complete whether the world exists or not. Creation does not change God. It brings into existence what is not God. The universe is not God. Or as Sokolowski says, "God is not the top-most part of the universe." He is outside the universe. But the origin of the universe or cosmos is not itself. It has a purpose. Basically, this purpose is that other free and rational beings participate in the inner life of the Godhead.

This was the initial purpose of creation. From the beginning, God did not create a universe then wonder what to put in it. Rather, the cosmos was the result of His original intention. Man was to achieve something that was in fact beyond his given nature. No purely natural man ever existed. None exists now. We are all imbued with Augustine's "restless hearts" that will never allow us to be satisfied with anything other than the original purpose of our creation. The history of the cosmos and the history of revelation as related to it is the explanation of how this purpose is to be carried out in the light of man's free will.

Q. #3): (CH) What do you mean by the notion that the human mind should be open to the whole of reality? In your *Modern Age*, you talk about the basic evidence that is often lost today. What is this basic evidence?

A. #3): (JVS) A good place to begin to think about such a question is with E. F. Schumacher's little book, *A Guide for the Perplexed*. This is a very brief and insightful sketch of how modern notions of certitude and methodology combined to limit our insight into reality, to what could be known by what is called "scientific method." Essentially, if something cannot be "proved" by this method, almost always itself something that presupposes quantity, the conclusion follows that it does not exist. By this method we cannot "prove" that we ourselves exist. The ways we know the most important things are rarely based on scientific method, yet we know them. We know that our mother loves us, but there is no way to "prove" it.

The word "proof" technically means to begin with something that is known for certain and proceed by logical steps to conclude to something that is not yet known. But all proof depends on something that is known by itself, for its own sake. We reach the foundation of proof when we grasp the meaning of the principle of contradiction. Even if we verbally deny the proposition, we implicitly affirm it by claiming that our position is valid.

The definition of mind in Aristotle is that power in us that is capable of knowing all things, *all that is*. Our minds are open to the "whole" of what exists. This openness is why it is all right to be a human being. What is not ourselves is open to us, given to us, by the fact that we can know it. When we know something, it does not cease to be what it is. But we change. In knowing, we have both our being and intentionally the being of what is not ourselves. This is the real foundation of our dignity and indicates the purpose for which we exist, to know *what is*, including its cause, and to love its reality and the fact that we are included within it.

Q. #4): (CH) On faith and reason, you write in *The Modern Age* about basic evidence that is left out today. What do you mean by saying that the human mind should be open "to all reality"?

A. #4): (JVS) This question follows on the previous one. The human mind is "capable of knowing all things." But one can understand philosophy or science to mean that we can only "know" what we know by modern methodology. The methodology limits us to know what the methodology presupposes. Since we really know things with our intuition or general understanding, we in fact know more than what science knows by its methods. Moreover, revelation contains intelligibility. If we exclude the intelligibility of either of these sources, we are cutting ourselves off from the whole.

The issue of revelation is of particular importance. Faith, as least in Catholicism, is not considered to be "absurd" or idiotic. It is directed to intellect. That is to say, revelation is addressed to intellect when intellect is being most intellect. That is, when the human intellect actively knows all that it can know, it still recognizes that it does not possess a knowledge of the whole. Since many issues remain for it to answer, it is confronted with the issue of whether the "reason" that is found in revelation is not in fact posed precisely as an answer to the questions as posed by reason but which it cannot answer by itself.

When we say that something is posed by "faith" or "revelation," we do not mean that it is not intelligible. We may mean that it is not originally something that the human intellect was able to figure out by itself. But we do not mean that, once revealed, it becomes "irrational" or "unintelligible." We mean the opposite. We mean that it explains a link that we could not figure out, but one that needed some additional intellectual input to make complete sense. The revelation of the Trinity itself was precisely of this nature.

The validity of revelation itself, like all faith, depends on the testimony of someone who sees. Faith does not depend on faith *ad infinitum*. It reaches back finally to someone who in fact sees. So if there is a coherence between revelation and reason, it is because the same "seeing" is at the origin of both.

Q. #5): (CH) What exactly do you mean by the phrase "*what is*" that you often use in your writing?

A. #5): (JVS) Ultimately, I suppose, it comes from Plato, truth is "to say of *what is* that it is, and of what is not, that it is not." The phrase has two sides, the "what" side and the "is" side. The first step of the human mind when it knows is to note a "what," a "form," that is, this thing is not that thing. A cow is not a toad. The second issue, though it grounds all "what" things, is the "is." Does this thing stand out of nothingness? Is it there? We put the two together when we affirm that this (this what) exists. The "is" is Aquinas's "*esse*," the to be.

The passage from nothingness to an existing thing must be accomplished by the agency of something *that is*. Ultimately, this leads to a being whose "what" is an "is." This is the most basic understanding of God, whose being is not limited by any finite form. His being is His what. We seem to have arrived at this understanding with the help of revelation, especially the response of Yahweh to Moses who wanted to know what name to give Him. The answer was to tell the people that "I Am who am." The New Testament is filled with "I Am" statements on the part of Christ who thereby identifies Himself with the origin of being. These two strands meet when the philosopher, taking his thought to its limits, encounters the "I Am" as a response to the question of "why is there something rather than nothing?"

The significance of *what is*, I think, lies in the wonder we encounter when something not ourselves comes into our ken. Aristotle said that the beginning of our thinking is wonder, not some necessity or coercion. We just want to know what the thing is. We do not initially want to do anything with it. We have first to figure out what sort of a being it is. We act according to the nature of what we encounter. That is, we treat human beings differently from birds or rocks because of what they are. Moreover, we find a delight, a pleasure in just knowing that something is, what it is. We could never by ourselves concoct the variety of things *that are*. It is almost as if what is not ourselves is out there so that we might know it. In this sense, the reality that is not ourselves appears to us as a gift, not as some configuration of our own mind. If it were, we would soon be bored with it.

Q. #6): (CH) You have taught college undergraduates for many years. You know the intellectual tradition of the West in great minds and ideas through things we call books. What are the basic questions of meaning and purpose that every liberal arts student should consider?

A. #6): (JVS) Interestingly enough, sources as widely divergent as Leibniz, Eric Vogelin, and Vatican II give pretty much the same list. They would include: Why am I, rather than am not? Why am I this thing rather than that thing? Why must I die? Am I responsible for my thoughts and actions? Why am I the only kind of being in the universe whose ultimate perfection or goodness depends on himself, not instinct or someone else?

In the first chapter of book 19 of the *City of God*, Augustine affirms: "*Nulla est homini cause philosophandi nisi ut beatus sit*—No cause of philosophizing can be found for man other than that he be happy." The reason ultimately that we go to college is not to find jobs, learn some skill, or play around. No, we go so that, in our leisure, we might come to know ultimate things. What else that we do makes sense only if we have an understanding of what the whole is about and of our part within it. Never to reflect on the sources of wisdom, of *what is*, is to live an "unexamined life," a life that Socrates warned us not to live.

It is true, again to follow what Plato told us about the steps in our education in the sixth and seventh books of the *Republic* that when we are twenty or so, we only have begun. We have not yet the experience to be wise about the important things. And yet, as Aristotle told us, if we are brought up with good habits, when the important things come into our lives we will recognize them. We will know that some things contradict reason before we can articulate what the principle of contradiction is. We can look on human life as an adventure in the knowing *what is*. If we combine the notions of adventure and gift, we will come close to the spirit in which we should live our lives.

Finally, we should know something of evil and its origins. We should wonder about why evil things exist, especially in ourselves. But, in the end, all evil is found in some good. And as Augustine said, no evil would ever be allowed to be present in our lives unless, out of it, some greater good could, but need not, come forth.

I would not conclude by touching evil were it not the other side of our freedom. We really are responsible for ourselves and one another. We can choose to put an action in the world that lacks something that ought to be there. This is what evil is. God could not possibly invite beings to His inner Trinitarian life if they were not free to love Him. This is what the divine friendship is about. We may learn about it before we live it. But unless we live it, we will learn only about ourselves, not the *what is* that includes ourselves, the *what is* of the greater glory that includes *all that is*.

Chapter 16

"The most famous book in the history of economics was called 'The Wealth of Nations,' not 'The Poverty of Nations.'"

Interview by Matteo Matzuzzi (MM) from Il Foglio, Rome with James V. Schall, S.J., on eve of Pope Francis's visit to Cuba and the United States.[*]

Question #1): (MM) One of the words Pope Francis probably will use in the U. S. will be "poverty." He often relates this word to a great critic of capitalism. Is it correct, in your opinion, to propose this correlation?

Answer #1): (JVS) Pope Francis often asks people to tell him what they think is true, not what they think that he wants to hear. Otherwise, he cannot learn anything new. This is a fine quality.

The most famous book in the history of economics was called "The *Wealth* of Nations" not "The *Poverty* of Nations." In the beginning everyone was poor. The problem was not to explain why the poor were poor but why anyone at all was *not* poor. Generally speaking, the reason why anyone is not poor is because of capitalism understood as innovation, growth, profits, distribution, and productivity.

The Holy Father's use of the term "capitalism" usually strikes most Americans as an equivocal usage of the word in which something is being described of which we have little knowledge. The fact is that the percentage of poor in the world has steadily decreased in recent decades. This is too seldom acknowledged or explained. What prevents dealing with the remaining poor is usually not capitalism in any form but political or religious ideas and corruptions that work contrary to poverty alleviation.

The principal impediment to helping the poor is too often the policies of the modern state itself, especially varieties of open or covert socialism.

---

[*]   Interview on-line, www.ilfoglio.it, September 24, 2015.

Catholic social thought has but rarely recognized that governments them-selves, with their own kind of greed, are primary obstacles to helping the poor help themselves. Latin American economic ideas often seem to be a heritage of the mercantilism of the colonial period, more of a state monopoly capitalism than anything we recognize by that name. No one denies that abuses exist. We deal with the abuses to let the system do what it can best do.

Q. #2): (MM) Do you think the Pope's "apocalyptic narrative" will be understood by American society?

A. #2): (JVS) You mean by "apocalyptic narrative," presumably, what the Holy Father says about ecology? He describes a this-worldly narrative of disasters caused by "earth warming." I would suspect that practically all the "facts" on which this thesis are said to be based are challengeable on scientific and practical grounds. Any problems are mostly explained in terms of natural cycles and conditions in the sun and the planet. The records of recurrent "ice ages" and "milder ages" seem to be as old as the earth itself. The percentage of any problem caused by human activity seems relatively small and can be dealt with in terms of our knowledge and tech-nology. Some warming even seems beneficial.

If you mean, on the other hand, "apocalyptic narrative" in the sense of the Pope's oft-repeated reference to Robert Hugh Benson's *The Lord of the World*, which really does depict "end times," I suppose we have always to recall St. Paul's "We know not the day or the hour." Still, it does seem that we have now managed to overturn most of the basic principles of natural law in our public policies so that the modern state and culture often stand for just the opposite of what classic teaching has indicated. I think it is a duty of a pope to warn a world that is being formed against the explicit teachings of reason and the Gospel. All of this latter has little or nothing to do with ecology but everything with how we choose to live in whatever society we live.

Q. #3): (MM) The Catholic Church seems to emphasize that the poor are poor because the rich are rich. The rich are depicted as "great sinners." Why?"

A. #3:) (JVS) St. Augustine used to say that both the rich and the poor can sin or be virtuous. The rich man does not have to become poor to be virtuous, nor does the poor man have to become rich to be virtuous.

Aristotle said that most people need a certain sufficiency of goods to be virtuous. This is what true economic growth tries to achieve. Francis himself mentions rich friends of his who are good and generous men. Almost everyone recognizes that greed is a vice, though probably not as destructive as envy in the long run.

Aristotle also discussed this issue in terms of the virtues of justice and moderation. A rich man is not necessarily unjust because he is rich, nor is a poor man virtuous just simply because he is poor. Each can save or lose his soul in his present condition. Aristotle suggested that a wealthy man could do three things with his wealth. He discussed this in terms of truth, good, and beauty. He could establish a library, or a hospital, or an art museum. Thereby, he would return to the common good what he possessed. States which confiscate all wealth prevent such free activities from going on. The record of much voluntary philanthropy and charity confirms this view.

Even when we read the Bible, we have to wonder where the rich of that period acquired their wealth. We know where the poor came from. The wealthy didn't just steal it all. Was it always or necessarily acquired from exploitation? Take the parable of the talents. The man who has ten talents, because of his investment acquires another ten. He is praised for it. It is the man who does nothing with what he has been given who is chastised. Capitalism, at its best, is a system that universalizes these basic principles.

Scripture is not a textbook in economics. God did not reveal to us everything we need to prosper, only a couple of things that we could not figure out by ourselves. He gave us brains, hands, and time. He left us the responsibility of figuring out how we could provide for ourselves. If He gave us everything, why bother about creating us in the first place?

The discovery of how not to be poor on a worldwide basis is a discovery of modern times, but so is the state's discovery of a method to control all of human life. Indeed, most of the totalitarian movements of modern times were and are presented as ways to help the poor. The poor become subjects of ideological manipulation and self-justification. But I think that the rich, the poor, and all in-between need each other. Just as the poor "will always be with us" so will the rich and in-between. What they all need is growth. They also, more fundamentally, need a sense of virtue and mutual responsibility. When these latter are lacking, the rich and poor, as Plato also said, will see themselves as antagonistic to each other.

Q. #4): (MM) In your last book, *On Christians & Poverty*, you write that poverty is something to be removed by the poor themselves. The argument seems to me to be revolutionary. In the recent Magisterium, we hear the opposite—the rich have to help the poor. What do you think?

A. #4): (JVS) The notion that the poor should remove their poverty by themselves is simply another way of stating the famous principle of subsidiarity, namely, that what can be done at the lowest level should be done there.

I look on this issue in this way:

1) We want people to be not poor.
2) We want them to make their way in the world by their own enterprise.
3) Often, the poor do not know how not to be poor.
4) More often, their governments do not know how either.
5) The poor can only learn how not to be poor from those who have learned how not to be poor.
6) No one will become not poor unless he has an incentive to do so.
7) The difference between successful and unsuccessful nations in the matter of poverty alleviation is measured by the degree to which they have learned how freedom, property, market, enterprise, rule of law, and virtue belong together.

The notion that wealth is a service means that the ways to be not poor, which most people desire and can learn, are made available through education, example, and, yes, by the competition found in market mechanisms. One of the great contributions of capitalism was the notion that a failed business did not condemn the owner to slavery, as is implied in some of the Gospel parables.

What works and what does not work are still issues. What works should be rewarded; what does not work should cease. The government should not be involved in keeping in business by taxing those enterprises that do not work. Those who need help should be given help by those who know how to help. No one wants a doctor to help him if the doctor does not know what is wrong with him. The whole point of a free market is to allow the poor not to be poor by themselves, by their own enterprise.

The trouble is, too often, that many want the poor to be poor and remain poor so that their own theories or projects can be justified in the name of helping the poor. The last thing the poor need is advice from someone, including the government and religion, who does not know how to help them. This is the danger that many good people fall into when thinking about the poor.

Q. #5): (MM) Another issue in your book is that inequality is not injustice. Can you explain this in a few words?

A. #5): (JVS) It is closer to the truth to say that "equality is injustice" than to say that "inequality is injustice." When God created the hierarchy of angels, he created each differently. It was not an injustice to the cow that it is not a horse or an angel. This is all in Aquinas. If everything is equal, then no distinction can be found in things.

The whole meaning of a "common good" is that a wide variety of different goods exists, some more important than others. But all are needed in order that the greatest good, the whole, be achieved. The eye does not want the foot to be an eye. It wants it to be a foot. The variety of talent, virtue, energy, and intelligence is a good, not a bad thing. If we try to make everything "equal," if, for instance, we give every student the same grade no matter what his performance, we simply destroy any standard of better and worse. Most efforts to improve would cease. If someone runs a hundred-meter dash faster than I do, I am not being treated unjustly, but justly. It would be unjust for me to claim to be his equal in this matter.

This same thing is true in the economic and political world. We need and want a variety of different capacities and talents that are brought together not to make everyone equal but to allow us to specialize and do what we could not otherwise have done. If I am so equal that I must do everything by myself, I end up by living in a primitive way as I can only do a few things by myself. Inequality is unjust only when it does not deny the truth of real differences among us that need to be what they are in order to be at all. These differences are so designed that we have a variety and abundance in which everyone can participate through exchange, markets, or generosity. Basically, this is what Aristotle's treatment of commutative and distributive justice was about.

Chapter 17

INTERVIEW ON ULTIMATE ISSUES WITH KATHRYN LOPEZ*

"Not to be able just to get up and go someplace under one's own power any time of day or night is an abiding penance. Leisurely walking has been a defining joy of my life. Many people, you really cannot help but notice, have it much worse than you. But that does not allow you to forget that it is you who must live with and cope with what you have left. And what you have left is still you. The famous question posed to everyone, of whether he would like to be someone else besides the person he already is can be answered briefly—'No'!"

Responses to Questions Posed by Kathryn Lopez
January 15, 2019

Question #1: Kathryn Lopez (KL) What is it like to have been on the brink of death and come back?

Answer #1: James V. Schall, S.J. (JVS) It turns out that I was not really at the brink of death, though I thought that I was. The agonizing problem was with a twisted colon, which was repaired by the operation. The doctors figured that I would pull through. On the other hand, when I asked in the hospital for no more extraordinary means, there was talk of infection and a second operation. At the time, I assumed that it was good-bye Schall to this world in a few days. I expected to be in hospice care, but that was not needed.

The "coming back" was sobering when I realized the impediments that are given to one's mobility as a result of this type of operation. Not to be able just to get up and go someplace under one's own power any time of day or night is an abiding penance. Leisurely walking has been a defining

---

* Published in www.crux.com, January 29, 2019.

joy of my life. Many people, you really cannot help but notice, have it much worse than you. But that does not allow you to forget that it is you who must live with and cope with what you have left. And what you have left is still you. The famous question posed to everyone, of whether he would like to be someone else besides the person he already is can be answered briefly—"No!"

Q. #2: (KL) Did you feel a little like Lazarus? Like the resurrected Christ?"

A. #2: (JVS) Well, both Lazarus and Christ were really dead. While I was in bad shape as I thought, once conscious, I was quite sure the same old Schall was there, minus a few feet of intestine or whatever they took out.

Lazarus went on to die in this world, so his first sojourn in the world of death was brief compared to his second one. His coming back to life had a particular function or purpose in Christ's teaching. Christ had power over life and death. This power could not be simply a human accomplishment of medicine, technology, or anything else. What we know about it depends on the testimony of the people who were there. They clearly knew he was dead, but Christ brought him back, much to their astonishment.

The rising of Lazarus immediately raised the question: Who is it who exercises such power? We are easily recognize that it was not just another human power. That was the point. Those present were faced with a fact and a logic. We need to recall in this context the story of Dives in hell. He wanted to send a message to his brothers about his situation so that they could avoid it. He is told that the gulf is too wide and, even if a message did get to his brothers, they would not believe him. They already had Moses and the prophets. A direct message from the realm of the dead would not change their ways.

We think of the resurrection of Christ as the restoration of His life in its divine and human wholeness. We cannot really "feel" the way He did. What we can do, however, is to see that, once dead, what we long for is the restoration of our being following the reality of Christ's own resurrection. We want what it is that constitutes what we ourselves are. We too seek to pass over into the eternal life that we have been promised in the resurrection of Christ.

I always like to recall Aristotle here. He was clear that we are not just bodies or just souls but one being in which all things are ultimately ordered to the end of knowing *all that is*. Aristotle did not possess any intimation of resurrection. He did give us the understanding of what it is that is resurrected if it happens in some as yet unknown order.

Q. #3: (KL) Why do you think you keep keeping on? What is God trying to teach you? What might He be trying to teach the rest of us?

A. #3: (JVS) What a quaint phrase—"keep keeping on"! Be danged if I know. If you find yourself living and breathing, it means that you keep on living the already extended life you began at your conception. In a wonder about which Chesterton often referred, we had nothing to do with our initial coming to be. All that we have, we have received. Our lives seem to be gifts that make us wonder about the giver.

"What is God trying to teach you?" The question does cause one to realize that something may well be left to learn. I did figure that I had said, and said often, all that I had to say in this world. I do not feel like Augustine, who, at the end of his life, spent some time retracting his errors. I do not mean that Schall had no errors to retract or even that it might not be good to point them out.

The notion that God is trying to teach us something is no doubt valid. He is trying to teach us who He is as seen in the ongoing stream of our life. In reading the newspapers of late, I was struck that the local papers no longer feature obituaries. They all have 'life stories.' A long or brief account, usually with photo, of each person who has died is given. We wonder what the Lord taught each of them and if they learned what He had in mind. Somehow, when you read these life stories, you get the feeling something is left out. And there is something left out. It is the judgment of each person's life. We are not complete until we know our end.

In teaching one, all are taught. One of the saints, on confronting some great sin or evil, would say, "There but for the grace of God go I." I think God does teach us this way. We learn not only from our own situation, but from that of others. But our "life story" goes on until it ends. God intended that we all choose, by the way we live, to accept the eternal life for which He has created us and offered to us. The drama of each human life is centered in this choice to accept or reject the eternal life offered to it.

Q. #4: (KL) Why do you keep writing? Why don't you give yourself a break?

A. #4: (JVS) Well, writing is the one thing that I can still seem to do, though with restrictions due to sight and ability to get at texts and other sources that arouse one's interest. One usually keeps on doing what he has done, when possible. Writing is in most ways an acquired habit. Keep on writing is like keep on breathing. It keeps you alive.

But I admit there is a time to sow and a time to reap, a time to write, a time to be silent. One can at some time be content that he has said all he has to say. This way of approaching things gets back to the notion that our lives are encased in stories that end when we finally end. I think of W. C. Fields's tombstone: "All things considered, I'd rather be in Philadelphia." This inscription is doubly amusing because, in Fields's time, Philadelphia was considered the most boring of places to be.

Our words last longer than we do. In any case, I prefer to think that I give myself a break by writing rather than not writing. However, a case may be made that my readers, if any, might need a break. We still retain the freedom of choosing what we read and what we pass over. The function of a writer is to make it difficult to pass his words over.

Q. #5: (KL) What do you want the world to consider about St. Ignatius, if it's a last prod from one of his Jesuit sons?

A. #5: (JVS) Ignatius taught us to be alert to the ongoing drama of human life as its details unfold before our very eyes in this vast cosmos in which we find ourselves. When we look at the world, we do not see only the world, however much we insist that such is all that we see. We see some rising and others falling. We see fame and pettiness. We are to discipline ourselves so that we see what is there, not what we would like to be there.

If we consider that perhaps 100 billion people have already lived on this planet, we cannot but wonder how it all fits together not merely in numbers but in intertwined stories of individual lives. Ignatius was not afraid to consider the reaches of Hell and what it might mean to find one's self or others there. But this consideration is the obverse side of our freedom that orders us to see the wonder in all existing things and in what happens to them.

The Jesuit motto, *in actione contemplativus*, contemplation in action, has always made sense to me. It can be used as an excuse not to consider the transcendent order, grace, and sacrifice; but in itself it makes one aware that an order of grace and providence is present among us. God not only created the world, but He keeps in existence and governs it for the purpose of His initial decision to invite other free and rational beings (angels and men) to participate in His inner, eternal life. We do also contemplate the rise and fall of nations and men. No story is insignificant. Our own story is interwoven with the stories of others.

Action refers to our doing and making things. These too are worthy of our attention. Indeed, the very first act of our mind in knowing is contemplative. The first thing we do is to behold, know what is there. Only then can we properly act upon it. We not only need to pray, we need to act, to rule ourselves. We need to be free to be what we are. We are the only being whose perfection (or degradation) also depends on itself. And all of this self-rule takes place in the context of ourselves immersed in a world of others with whom we must deal.

But in the end, I find myself constantly returning to Ignatius's principle: "Man was made to praise, reverence, and serve God, and by this means to save his soul. And the other things in the world are given to him to use for his ultimate purpose. Hence, he is to use them or not use them according as they lead him to the end for which he was created." We are involved in the saving of our own souls, in the final purpose of our life. And Ignatius's saving does not just run through ourselves but through our dealings with others in the world in which we find ourselves. We are not asked to live someone else's life, only our own. We are asked, yes "prodded," to live our own life for the end for which it is called out of nothing in the first place."

Q. #6: (KL) You gave a "Last Lecture" in Gaston Hall (youtube/schall/lastlecture/georgetown). Is there anything you might add?

A. #6: (JVS) No, I am content with what was found in that lecture. It is not good form to have more than one "last lecture." That lecture had to do with my life as a teacher amidst many of the several thousand students I had in various classes over the years of my tenure at Georgetown. No professor can be indifferent to what his students have taught him. I followed the observation of Frederick Wilhelmsen that a professor is not a professor unless he finally set down for his students and for the public what it is that he has learned in his time in academia. The "Last Lecture" was my effort to fulfill this welcome admonition.

That being said, I have wanted to make two short texts in which I summarize or account for how I understand the heart of Christian revelation and what I think is the major insight into political philosophy that is found in my sundry writings.

Q. #7: (KL) In your most recent e-mail, you noted Msgr. Robert Sokolowski at Catholic University as one of the best minds we have today in the Church. Why is that? What do we all have to learn from him?

A. #7: (JVS) Msgr. Sokolowski is a good friend. I had come across his work only later in life and have often spoken with or written to him. His books and thought reveal a clarity of thought and a carefulness and attention to reality for which he gives a lucid and penetrating account. His life work has been to show how the work of Husserl relates to Aquinas and the core of Western thought.

At first sight, his body of publications is formidable. The best single philosophy book I know, one that step-by-step takes the reader through every essential phase of human thought is found in his book *The Phenomenology of the Human Person*. He wanted to entitle this book, "The Agent of Truth," a far better title, but the publishers (Cambridge) thought it sounded too much like a detective story! It begins with his oft-repeated principle that the first act of the mind is contemplative and wants first to distinguish clearly what is found not first in the mind but in reality. His book breaks every issue down to intelligible parts which build on each other. No book is quite like it.

Sokolowski knows his history of thought, the connection of ideas, and modern thought on basic issues. His book *The God of Faith and Reason* is the place to begin reading him. His fundamental idea that God is not "part" of the world develops into an understanding of creation as something that exists but need not, and thus requires an origin that is transcendent to the given cosmos in which we find ourselves.

Sokolowski's book *Christian Faith & Human Understanding* is a series of profound essays on a number of theological and moral principles. His discussion of a vocation like medicine or any of the professions is really outstanding. He also recognizes in his book *Pictures, Quotations, and Distinctions* that we do not just learn by words (a central topic of his *Phenomenology of the Human Person*). His book *Eucharistic Presence* lays out the whole issue of the Eucharist in all its philosophical and theological overtones. Each year or so he has taken a class through his commentary on Aristotle's *Politics* and its abiding ramifications. All of this is in addition to his work on

Husserl, the basic lines of which are found in his book, *An Introduction to Phenomenology*.

In brief, I would affirm that no one can take us to the heart and essentials of the complete truth of things faster than Sokolowski. But when you finally read him, he demands attention, he incites your wonder. Truth does not exist except when it is actively affirmed in a mind that knows of *what is* that it is.

Q. #8: (KL) Are you sad that things are being revealed about the church, McCarrick, and all, things happening in your sunset years?

A. #8: (JVS) Needless to say! I am not so much sad that they are revealed as I am that they happened. I have always been Augustinian enough to know that such things have and do happen. We are a sinful lot and sometimes enjoy the sins of others to escape zeroing in our own. But this situation involves the very highest reaches of the Church including the papacy itself. Where the Holy Spirit in all of this is to be found is by no means clear. Our presumption that Rome would always be there to back reason and the essentials of revelation can be shaken. People rightly lose confidence when they see the Church identified as a place of abusers at the highest levels.

So it is unsettling not to know what must come of all of this. For not a few, it proves that the Church cannot be what it said it was. For others, it is a question of enforcing honesty about the facts and the recognition of the enormous results of scandal and aberrant human behavior, especially among the clergy. And the same problems arise not just among Catholics but, though not acknowledged, are found widespread in the public order. We now have an intrinsic double standard, as it were. The public law tells us that homosexuals have a right to do whatever they do (except prey on minors), whereas the natural law sees these ways of life as disordered. I found Jennifer Roback Morse's recent book, *The Sexual State*, to be a remarkable insight into the basic issues at stake here.

The papacy often seems, as Daniel Mahoney recently put it in his book, *The Idol of the Age*, to embrace many of the principles of secular humanism. Certainly the atmosphere of so many of the appointments and documents is to the left and far left of the social and political spectrum, to advocate as norms things that have always failed in practice. The clarity and insights that were so abundant during the time of Paul VI, John Paul II, and

Benedict are silenced or bypassed. I have not forgiven Benedict for resigning! That being said, to cite John XXIII, "Corragio"; it is not over yet. The principle that all evils bear some good in them out of which good can come remains valid.

Q. #9: (KL) Why have you, at least as long as I have been reading your emails, signed off with the request: "Pray for me"?

A. #9: (JVS) First of all, it is because I do want people to pray for me. Lord knows that I need all the help I can get and the help of the Lord is something basic that we are to ask for from one another. The classic response in the litany is *Ora pro nobis*. Pray for me is simply the same response in singular.

One does get some various responses. One will wonder if I am not in some kind of personal crisis. Another will assure me that he does not pray, but wishes me well. Most will not comment, or say, "Pray for me too." Some types of letters do not include it—letters of recommendation for student applications, for example. But personal letters usually do include it. It assumes that everyone prays for something, even if they do not. We might as well include Schall in the mix.

Q. #10: (KL) What is best about life?

A. #10: (JVS) What is best about life? The first thing is having it, actually being in existence and knowing that we exist as this human being, that we do not cause ourselves to exist. We are given life. What is best about life is to know that it is a gift rather than some blind development with no internal meaning to itself as this, and not that, being.

Following on this realization of our own existence, what is best is knowing that we are not alone. We live among others and seek and rejoice in our friends. We discover in revelation that we are also to become friends of God. Our lives are often filled with sin and suffering, when we need others most for forgiveness, for help, for understanding.

What is best about life is also the fact that we can walk this green earth, see things, and especially know what ourselves is *not*. We exist also that what is not ourselves in all its variety and complexity can be known to us. We are not deprived of the world or others because we are not they. Instead in knowledge, the world and our friends return to us. We know a world that is not ourselves; we are blessed.

Q. #11: (KL) What is most challenging about life?

A. #11: (JVS) Finding its order. My book, *The Order of Things*, goes into this issue. At first sight, the world seems a chaos, a disorder. But the earth and all in it reveal an order that is not there because *we* put it there. We find it already there. This is what we discover when we discover anything.

Modern (and Muslim) voluntarism will claim that nothing is stable (an old Greek view also). Everything can be its opposite. Therefore, there are no evils. But there are evils, due precisely to a lack of order. Moral evil is a lack of order that we put in our own thoughts and deeds because we reject that order that is given to us that constitutes our own real good. The challenge of life is to deal with the reasons for evil without despair or without affirming that evil is good.

Even in the worst circumstances, we strive to see what is in order. But when it is our responsibility to affirm or allow that order, we can prefer our own ideas. In doing so, we implicitly reject the being *that is*. Thanks to the redemption, this rejection can be repented and reordered, but even here we are required to act in a way that confronts what is really wrong. We are responsible for our own lives. In the end, the story of our personal existence will be told in terms of how we lived and understood the gift of life that we have been freely given.

Q. #12: (KL) What's most unappreciated about life?

A. #12: (JVS) In a way, I suppose it has to do with what Aristotle said was the beginning of our knowledge, namely, our capacity to wonder. Samuel Johnson (whose life is simply one of amazing wonder) cautioned that we are not to go about just wondering. We are to learn and come to conclusions. We are to know the truth of things, we in our very own minds. But we are provoked by what is not ourselves. What is out there beyond our ken? We are not content simply to say "I do not know or want to know." We come to full knowledge only gradually. And we never cease to wonder about what is out there even when we know something about it.

So I would say that what is most unappreciated about life is the adventure of it, the sense that it is really going someplace and this lovely world is not its ending but beginning. In addition, we do not appreciate how much we can damage ourselves and others when we do not know the truth of things and reject the order of things to impose our own order on our lives and world. We have been redeemed, but we have not been excused in our freedom. We are not able to be friends with one another or with God unless we choose, by the way we finally live, to do so.

Q. #13: (KL) What is the most important gift of your life, besides life itself? Your priesthood? The Sacraments?

A. #13: (JVS) I have long said, and urged the point on anyone who will listen, that the best thing that our parents give us is brothers and sisters, and eventually along with their children. Even if my two good brothers are with the Lord, their welcome to me and our own hassles have been a context of life that has always been a consolation to me. My good sister and my two step-sisters are also here.

"Of course, priesthood and sacraments, the life of the Church as I have been given in the Society of Jesus loom large. The Order in my time has provided me with education and opportunity that I could not otherwise imagine for a young man from a small town in Iowa. I have lived for a time in some great cities—San Francisco, Rome, Washington. But the great gift to me was the chance to live a life relatively free to read and write and wonder how it all fit together. I have never been a "specialist," and it probably shows, but I have thought often about the whole. I think that leisure to wonder about what it is all about has been a great gift to me.

I have loved teaching and the students that somehow kept coming to my often-meandering classes in which I was often but one step ahead of them, and not always then. Indeed, having young men and women there, to tell them just what there is to be read that will open their eyes to *what is*, has been part of this gift. If I could entice but one student to read *Joseph Pieper–an Anthology* or E. F. Schumacher's *A Guide for the Perplexed*, I would be happy with the chance of being there to see the delight the student saw on actually reading these good books, or Plato or Aristotle or Augustine or Aquinas or Johnson.

Q. #14: (KL) Are you ready? And how do you know that you are?

A. #14: (JVS) At 91, one has little leeway. The old hide-and-seek cry, "Here I come, ready or not," is in place. We do not know the day or hour. So we abide in what is given to us in the now. We do not know if we are "ready"; we just try to be, to have faith and courage. If we had certitude about these things, we would already be dead.

Q. #15: (KL) Are there any last words that you might like to add in the unlikely event that this isn't your last interview?

A. #15: (JVS) What an amusing way to put it! The "unlikely event"! Yes, Schall can be long-winded. I noted the other day that the complete listing of what I have published according to date and source since my first essay in *The Commonweal*, in 1954, comes to about 150 pages. This includes books, book reviews, chapters in books, academic essays, columns, lighter and shorter essays, interviews, letters to editors, and newspaper essays. Indeed, St. Augustine's Press is yet to publish one of these days a collection of my earlier JVS interviews.

I think that my last words remain those that I cited from Chesterton at the end of the "Last Lecture"—that all inns lead to that Great Tavern at the end of the world when we shall drink again with our friends in that eternal life that is offered to us by our very God when he called each of us out of nothing to exist and participate in His inner life.

The Trinity has always fascinated me. A chapter in my first book, *Redeeming the Time*, was entitled: "The Trinity—God Is Not Alone." Aristotle wondered if God was lonely and therefore lacked one of the highest of human values. Since there is otherness, love, and inner-relationship in God, He does not need the world to explain his glory. The world as we know it reflects His glory, but His glory as it is awaits us. Our lives transcend the world, even while we remain in this world, with all its own tragedy, drama, and uncertainties. The last words remain—we are bound for glory, *Deo Gratias*!

Conclusion

"THE NEAREST NOTION OF PARADISE"

"Groping for something that would satisfy, he (Stevenson) found nothing so solid as that fancy. That had not been Nothing; that had not been pessimistic; that was not a life over which Lazarus could do nothing but weep. That was as positive as paints in the paint-box, and the difference between vermillion and chrome yellow. Its pleasures had been as solid as the taste of sweets; and it was nonsense to say that there had been nothing to them worth living for. Play at least is always serious. So long as we can say, 'Let's pretend,' we must be sincere. Therefore he appealed across the void or valley of his somewhat sterile youth to that garden of childhood, which he had once known and which was his nearest notion of paradise."
—G. K. Chesterton, *Robert Louis Stevenson*, CW, XVIII, 82–83.

Boswell, as we saw in the beginning citation to the Introduction, was concerned with the "cloudy darkness" of his own mind. He was afraid that the darkness was perhaps preferable to light, to the gift and capacity to see what is given to us. Stevenson, as Chesterton tells us, understood that "fancy" was better than a world with no hope. He was not a nihilist. He saw that solid things were indeed solid. He saw that vermillion and chrome yellow were real colors. The garden of his childhood reflected the Garden of the breezy afternoon before Adam discovered the unclad condition in which he freely placed himself.

We have seen throughout the course of these interviews, I hope, that the informality of this literary form allows us to speak of things that would not be allowed or expected in more "academic" journals or ordinary courses offered to students who are told that they are still being "educated" even without them. Sometimes students believe it. But hopefully a touch of "fancy" remains in their souls. It is not without interest that one of the main themes of modern thought, if not the main theme, is the location of paradise, however it is called. Is it on this earth as a result of man's own making, or is it something transcendent, a gift related, no doubt, to what is done in this world, but still not the same?

In reflecting on the nature of "interviews," we recall that both John Paul II in his *Crossing the Threshold of Hope* and Joseph Ratzinger in his *Salt of the Earth*, *Milestones*, and the *Ratzinger Report*, used the interview format with great effectiveness. As we noted, it is already an element in the understanding of Pope Francis. An interview, to be sure, has nowhere near the authority of an encyclical or apostolic letter. The press conference of a President or Prime Minister does not carry the same weight as his more official pronouncements. Still, as we see, the interview succeeds in opening to us something of the person that we might not otherwise have noticed.

The value of the interview can, perhaps, be seen in the response that Josef Ratzinger gave in an interview with the Italian journalist, Vittorio Messori. They had been discussing the very issue that Chesterton saw in Stevenson. Ratzinger recognized that modern thought is often a reconstruction of what are in effect Christian ideas, only now transposed and geared to this world and its condition.* "The 'absolute good' (and this means the building of a just socialist society) becomes the moral norm that justifies everything else including—if necessary—violence, homicide, mendacity."* The end-good is seen as so important and urgent that no restrictions on it are allowed in its pursuit.

Actually, all this has already been described in the first pages of the Bible. The core temptation of man and his fall is contained in this programmatic statement: "You will be like gods" (Genesis 3:5), Ratzinger explains to Messori. "Like God, that means free of the Law of the Creator, free of the law of nature herself, absolute lord of one's own destiny. Man continually desires only one thing: to be his own creator and his own master. But what awaits us at the end of the road is certainly not Paradise."*

---

*   See James V. Schall, *The Modern Age* (South Bend: St. Augustine's Press, 2011).

*   *The Ratzinger Report: An Exclusive Interview* (San Francisco: Ignatius Press, 1985), 91.

*   Ibid.

That we can come across such a passage in an interview, one that puts us in mind of other elements of our literary inheritance, is itself, in my view, sufficient justification for a collection of essays. Hopefully, the reader will find contained herein at least some touch with reality that causes him to wonder about these things, to wonder about what is true, to wonder why some notions of Paradise turns out to be its opposite.

In following these interviews, as I have said, the reader will come across "just about everything" or, as the old song went, he will find "a little bit about a lot of things." One might say that a fundamental difference can be detected between important and unimportant things. And I will accept this distinction provided that we recognize that even the most insignificant thing can lead us to anything, even to the cause of *what is*. We are not only surrounded by important things. We are surrounded by everything. Both seem to have the same sources.

These interviews are to be seen in the light of "a breezy afternoon in a Garden." The most momentous of things can happen at any time and anywhere. The ordinary things do happen every day around us. The problem with human life, as I think these interviews remind us, is not that there is too little to know, but too much. And this brings us back to Boswell's concern with the "dark" thought that if we know too much, we might lose all the mystery of things.

I hope these interviews reveal, as Boswell put it, "to the thinking part of my readers" that we need not, indeed we cannot, exhaust the mystery of things. When we know all that there is to know about God, as Aquinas taught us, we know what He is not, not *what He is*. After the "final interview," if we be judged worthy, we do see, as St. Paul said, and we hope, "face-to-face." We are, as Adam found out and Plato taught, beings who are "interviewed," not just judged. This condition is what Tolkien called our "doom." It is also, in the end, our "glory."